Silent Terror

Silent Terror

A Journey into Contemporary African Slavery

SAMUEL COTTON

HARLEM RIVER PRESS

Published for Harlem River Press
by Writers and Readers Publishing, Inc.
P.O. Box 461, Village Station
New York, NY 10014

Writers and Readers Limited
36 Britannia Row
London N1 8QH
England

*Silent Terror: A Journey into Contemporary African Slav*ery
©1998 by Samuel Cotton

Book and cover design: Renée Michaels Design

ISBN # 0-86316-259-2 Trade Paper
 2 3 4 5 6 7 8 9 0

Manufactured in the United States of America

◈ Acknowledgements ◈

Although I have the privilege of being the author of Silent Terror, in reality, it is the product of many forces, and I wish to acknowledge those
forces, both spirit and flesh, who made it all possible.

I give thanks to my ancestors, who suffer because their children are still
suffering, for giving me the protection, courage, and guidance to bear witness. Appreciation for the courage of Dr. Charles Jacobs, Mohamed Athie
and Tony Brown which resulted in the issue of slavery being brought to the
attention of the public and to Andrew C. Cooper and Maitefa Angaza of
the black New York weekly newspaper, *The City Sun,* for the courage to
address this controversial issue. Thanks to Margaret Briggs for her selfless
devotion and support in the early days of the movement without which my
early abolition activities would have been impossible and to Robin Briggs
for her camera which captured the images of slavery. Thanks to Mansour
Kane and El Hadj Demba Ba who organized and financed the research trip
to Africa from their personal savings, Mocktar Toumbo for his help in
procuring a visa and Ba Mamadou Bocar and Abdoulaye Sy for their love
and protection. I will never forget Omar Ba, and Bocar Almamy Ba for their
invaluable friendship and research support, Samba Thiam president of the
African Liberation Forces of Mauritania for mission support and Amadou
Boubou Niang for seeking to make me comfortable in the refugee camp
N'dioum. May Allah give peace to Houleye Sall, the mother of a murdered
son, and president of The Widows for her help in understanding the pain of
the Negro-African women of Mauritania. My deepest appreciation to the
men and women in Mauritania who made this mission possible: To Hapsa
Dia and Sitty Haidara the most courageous women I have ever met, and
Fara Ba and Ibrahima Sarr.

Insights into slave life would have been impossible without the voices of
courageous anti-slavery leaders Boubacar Messaoud, and Messaoud Ould
Boulkheir. Thank you Leidji Traore for arranging and translating interviews
and to those still in bondage who courageously allowed me to interview

them: Brahim ould Maboune, Shaba mint Bilal, M'Barka Mint Bilal, Jebada Mint Maouloud and Aïchanna Mint Abeid Boilil. Thanks to the great Mauritania scholar and freedom fighter Garba Diallo for his research and insights into Mauritanian culture and history, Janet Fleishman of Human Rights Watch/Africa for her excellent research and to the researchers at Amnesty International.

Thank you Dr. John Henrik Clark for encouraging me to write this book because you believed that black people needed to understand this issue. To my spiritual brother and friend Amargi Uhuru (Sylvester Johnson) thank you for your encouragement and vision during my periods of utter exhaustion and despair. Thank you Lorena Parrish for your editorial guidance and direction in the early stages of the book and for demanding of me what I thought I did not have. To my editor Kamili Anderson, I have no words to express my appreciation for the professionalism, sensitivity and firm hand with which you guided and directed the editing process. Thank you Debra Dyson, for your marketing expertise, spiritual support and friendship. And Glenn Thompson of Harlem River Press, thank you my friend for having the vison and courage to publish this work.

❖   ❖   ❖

This book is dedicated to all those
who fight for a free Mauritania

AFRICA

Tunisia

Islas
Canarias (Sp.)

Morocco

Algeria

Libya

Egypt

Western
Sahara

Cape
Verde

Mauritania

Mali

Niger

Chad

Sudan

Eritrea

Djibouti

Somalia

Senegal

The Gambia

Guinea-
Bissau

Guinea

Sierra Leone

Liberia

Ivory
Coast

Burkina
Faso

Ghana

Benin

Togo

Nigeria

Cameroon

Central
African Rep.

Ethiopia

Equatorial
Guinea

Sao Tome
& Principe

Gabon

Congo

Democratic
Republic
of Congo

Uganda

Rwanda

Burundi

Kenya

Tanzania

Gulf of
Guinea

ATLANTIC
OCEAN

INDIAN
OCEAN

Angola

Zambia

Malawi

Mozambique

Zimbabwe

Namibia

Botswana

Swaziland

South
Africa

Lesotho

Cape of
Good Hope

◈ PREFACE ◈

It is foreboding that even as one reads the compelling revelations contained in *Silent Terror*, the daughters of Africa are routinely being subjected to slavery and its evil components of rape, torture, mutilation, and starvation. Disturbing as well is the finding that on the precipice of the twenty-first century, the sons of Africa continue to inherit the brutal legacy of their forefathers: castration, deprivation, bestialization, and oppression. For our sisters and brothers in slavery, today as in yesteryear, these abominations commence at birth and expire only upon death. As this book attests, these conditions in their modern form are the vile consequences of racialism and a multiracial caste system practiced under the substrate of colonialism. As they manifest themselves today on the continent of Africa, they are highly infectious sociopolitical diseases that further victimize and contaminate the mentality of hitherto oppressed people solely on the basis of their skin color. The pernicious policies and processes of Arabization and white hegemony upon the blacks of Africa—the true Africans, whom God blessed to be black—have resulted in blackness becoming an arbitrary curse.

There is a cruel contradiction to these hegemonic thought patterns, and it never ceases to amaze this author how the systematic expurgation of blackness factors into the historical recording of world events. For example, to those who are wedded to the strictest of racialistic world views, Arabs themselves are bracketed in the Africoid, not Caucasoid, racial category. One need only superficially peruse the historical genealogy of the Moors in the area under scrutiny in this work to discern that there is an undeniable miscegenistic connection between Africans and Arabs. Indeed, the term Moorisco is frequently applied to the people of Mauritania to reflect this linkage. It was the Moorisco Othello whose foibles Shakespeare so vividly characterized in his celebrated play. History also records that the Mooriscos were the group that challenged Christianity on the Barbary Coast—not the Arabs of cinematic fame in the film *Lawrence of Arabia*.

Yet, on the contemporary scene, Sam Cotton presents a case, beyond equivocation, that historians may endeavor to marginalize but that those who are committed to moral decency will memorialize and, I hope, rise up to counter and eradicate. Through rigorous application of journalistic proficiency, Cotton presents the bare-faced facts of contemporary racialism in yet another date and place on the African continent. In this instance, however, one cannot ascribe the provenance to Europeanism—at least not directly, although it is a known fact that France has played a dominant role in supporting the authoritarian rule of the violently insurgent president of Mauritania, Maaouya Ould Sid Ahmed Taya. The participating Arabs, for their part, erroneously abuse the doctrines of Islam in justification of the evils of slavery. Yet, anyone with even a surface acquaintance with the Holy Koran knows that slavery is not justified before Allah any more than it is warranted by the words of the Bible or in the eyes of the Christian God.

The Arabians' slavery of Africans continues to be timeless and incessant. It is among the most enduring crimes in human history, and it is the native and descendant Africans who continue to be perniciously victimized. To what extent has economic addiction degenerated the capacity among us all for compassion? How has it come to be that there is such precious little regard for the genocidal consequences that attend to slavery—in any form? Is the world not possessed of the moral fortitude or priority to end this most heinous form of racialism?

I have often been categorically assured by whites that had they lived during the time of the trans-Atlantic slave trade, they would have been on the side of the abolitionists. I have been assured in turn by blacks that had they themselves been among the enslaved of that era, they would have fought rebelliously for freedom. Well, certainly, as this book reveals, such an opportunity exists for blacks and whites today, but little hue and cry has been raised by either group. Still, the abolition of slavery does not beckon solely to persons of the same ethnic descent as the enslaved. It should beggar the world's collective sense of justice and every individual's capacity for reason to see such insouciance over the existence of slavery in the contemporary period.

In the resolution of this abomination, Muslim, Christian, and Judaic supporters must avoid the pitfall of religious presentimentality or vindictiveness. Good is good, and evil is evil. Nothing more and nothing less. Let us hope that the sentinel efforts of Samuel Cotton will be the initiative that succeeds in recapturing the world's regard for fundamental human decency. Through this documented exposure of the atrocities of slavery occasioned through the participation and condonation of the Arab populations of northern Africa, Sam Cotton has calibrated the world's moral compass. He reposes his ultimate confidence in the inexplicable justice that humanity has elected to barricade, but consequently must always entreat.

—THE REVEREND DR. JAMES V. MONTGOMERY, Esquire
First Governor, The World Federation for Uniracial Activism
New Haven, Connecticut

◆ PROLOGUE ◆

T*he white man killed my father*
Because my father was proud
The white man raped my mother
Because my mother was beautiful
The white man wore out my brother in the hot sun
of the roads
Because my brother was strong
Then the white man came to me
His hands red with blood
Spat his contempt into my black face
Out of his tyrant's voice:
"Hey boy, a basin, a towel, water."[1]
    —DAVID DIOP

It is December 23, 1995, and a steel ship, Flight 562, bound for Dakar, Senegal, surges and shudders in a storm somewhere over the Atlantic Ocean. Above me, a video screen begins to appear, opening slowly below the overhead luggage rack. The silent screen indicates the aircraft's progress by displaying a small plane moving slowly from the U. S. coastline to the west coast of Africa. As the screen flashes off and on, it appears to me, after two hours into the flight, that the small plane has hardly moved. Not being one who likes to sit for long periods of time, I tell myself to relax and accept that this is going to be a long flight. Anxious, I turn from the screen and begin to gaze out of the window.

My eyes follow the silver wings of the aircraft as they stretch proudly out into the frigid air, capturing and reflecting the sun's rays. I contemplate the soft appearance of the clouds and listen to the hum of the aircraft's engines. Gradually, the cloud cover begins to thin until it dissolves into a view of that great body of water known as the Atlantic Ocean.

For me, the water visible below is more than an ocean. It is a watery grave. A memorial. A liquid tombstone. In that gray expanse, below the white caps, lie millions of my ancestors who were either seduced by suicide's siren call, consumed by disease, or swallowed by storm-tossed seas with an appetite for wooden ships and their tormented cargo.

My thoughts, tranquil moments ago, fill with the history of a race jerked brutally off track—a race that has never recovered. My eyes mist as I contemplate the ocean and re-enter that space and time when my people were defeated and humiliated. I attempt to flee from these memories by turning away from the window and sinking back into my seat, but my spirit is locked in an embrace with the brutal past of my ancestors.

❋　　❋　　❋

I am not your usual passenger. No, the man of color seated in 22F is a traveler devoid of the usual enthusiasms, for I undertook this journey after being stripped of all my illusions. I am neither joyful nor expectant, nor am I one of those sentimental tourists on holiday, eagerly anticipating the sights and sounds of his first trip to Africa. Rather, I am surrounded by sadness, and in my manner there is a hint of fear.

I am a haunted man. Haunted by myriad thoughts that crawl in and out of my consciousness. Sometimes these thoughts dance quietly below the surface. Other times they burst forth loud and insistent, demanding attention. It is these thoughts, along with the ancestral whisperings, that are the force driving my trip. My reflections are the children of research, born in the early morning hours and dusky evenings of days lost listening to countless interviews of Africans caught in nightmarish circumstances.

The Africans I spoke to were from Mauritania and Sudan. Interviewing them meant hours of gazing into pained faces that related strange and terrible stories of human degradation and death. The written and oral evidence overwhelmed me. It was the evidence, after all, that took on a life of its own and commanded me to go to Africa.

Evidence, clear and insistent, that trading in black slaves was occurring in the North African countries of Mauritania and Sudan. Yes, Africa, in 1997, was still suffering from the same sickening humiliation that once almost destroyed her: human bondage. Her past was her present, and her present was her past.

THE LEGACY OF SLAVERY

I, like most African-Americans, have contended and wrestled for decades with a rage born of remembrance—a resentment fomented by the poignant images of Africans being captured, bound, and shipped into the

horrors of slavery. Many African-Americans have been driven by these images to travel to the shores of West Africa. They can be seen in Senegal
among the crowds at Gorée Island, standing in the "Doorway of No Return," or on the coast of Ghana, walking among the slave "castles." They
walk slowly and linger in the corners and stairwells of these hellish sites—
the terrible places where the degradation of a race began.

In these places, the great grandchildren of slaves, survivors of a holocaust, contend with a terrible mixture of emotions. Their passions are produced by the realization that the forts before them housed their shackled
ancestors in their last days on African soil before a long and miserable voyage delivered them into the hands of cruel masters. A wet eye, a sigh, and
then a wisp of white hot anger rises slowly within the hearts and minds of
these New World Africans as they recall these events. From the dark re-
cesses of their racial memories, storms appear on the psychic horizon. Epi-
thets begin to dance in their throats. Emotional forces take on a power of
their own and occasionally fight their way clear, escaping the lips as curses
and bitter mutterings.

Such acid expressions of resentment and grief can only be cooled and
soothed by a belief that many African-Americans hold: that the buying and
selling of black African slaves ended in the distant past. Such a belief, however, is both myth and illusion. I was cursed with the death of that illusion
in the year preceding this trip, when it became clear to me that the enslavement of black Africans did not stop with the demise of the trans-Atlantic
slave trade. The reality instead, I learned, is that on this very day and in this
very hour, even as you read these pages, black Africans are being bought and
sold in at least two northwestern African countries.

Today.

Now.

❁   ❁   ❁

The book you are about to read is a documented response to this atroc-
ity. It is an expression of moral outrage. It is an instrument designed to inform, to disturb, to prick the moral nerve of all who read it and, I hope,
elicit some moral reaction from the world community.

As a man of African descent, I am outraged that other African men and
women have been forced to live for centuries in a debased state as a result
of slavery and oppression. As a human being, I have a need to be reassured
of the world's humanity, a hunger to see some sign of moral indignation
over the continued enslavement and debasement of black people. It is espe-

cially important for me to see that those who worship Islam, whether they are white or black, say or do something about the abuse and enslavement of their black spiritual brothers and sisters. I pray that this book will be a means by which the ongoing enslavement of Africans will become an important issue, not only to them, but to all African-Americans, Americans, Africans, and other people around the world.

CHAPTER ONE

~~~~~~

I *am writing you to express my deep concern over the arrest in November and December 1990 of an estimated 3,000 Black Mauritanians, many of whom were allegedly tortured and held in extremely harsh conditions in military and police custody. Recent reports from Amnesty International and Agency France Presse state that approximately* **240 of the detainees died as a result of torture and ill-treatment.** *....In conclusion, I urge the Government of Mauritania to stop its persecution of individuals on the basis of race and to adhere to the international human rights conventions...*[1]
—RONALD V. DELLUMS, Member,
United States House of Representatives

I am not the only imam [Islamic religious leader] to be deported. Many other black imams have been deported. What is the most shocking is not that imams were deported, but the terrible abuses, the massacres, rape, and burning of homes, etc., against ordinary people who are Muslims and the violation to Islam itself.[2]
—IMAM MOHAMED EL FASO of Aleg, Mauritania

THE CITY SUN ASSIGNMENT

Flight 562 hits another pocket of air and drops. I become uneasy, nervous, and my thoughts return to home. It will be Christmas in two days, and I wonder what it will be like spending it in an unfamiliar place without my family. I ask myself, "Sam, do you really know what you are doing? Should you really be on this airplane?" To answer, I summon memories of how this all began.

It started one Saturday morning in 1994 as Andrew Cooper, the president of New York's *City Sun* Publishing Company sat watching a broadcast of "Tony Brown's Journal." The popular PBS show was featuring a program on modern-day slavery in Africa. Dr. Charles Jacobs, a Jewish-American human rights activist, and Mohamed Nacir Athie, a former Mauritanian diplomat now in exile in the United States, were Brown's guests. The two men belonged, at that time, to an organization called the American Anti-Slavery Group, and they were charging that Arab enslavement of black Africans could still be found in the artificially created country of Mauritania, approximately four hundred kilometers north of the infamous slave-holding pens on Gorée Island, and in battle-torn Sudan.[3]

Andrew Cooper wanted these allegations researched. He turned the project over to his executive editor, Maitefa Angaza, a bright and pleasant-spirited black woman who always had an encouraging word for her writers. Maitefa, an excellent writer, with a solid grasp of social issues, had recently replaced Stephanie Zinerman, who gave me my first chance to write for the *Sun*.

I was a graduate student at the time, attending Columbia University's School of Social Work. I was majoring in social research because I believed that, by doing so, I could make an intellectual contribution to the black community. Like a number of my peers, I also believed that black newspapers too often lacked the sophistication and depth—the *will*—to provide the critical analysis of events that our people sorely needed. After I had turned in a number of assignments to Maitefa, she came to share Stephanie's positive view of my work. My name soon appeared on the paper's masthead as a contributing writer.

I was determined to provide the *City Sun* with well-written and well-researched articles that would enable black Americans to better understand and respond to the complex web of social forces that plagued us. Maitefa had given me a number of opportunities to do so. She would call me when there was a special piece she wanted researched and developed into an article or series of articles. When I did not hear from her for a week or so, I would initiate the call.

It was on such a day, a bitterly cold day in December, that my life was to change forever. I hurried from class to the telephones located in the student center and called in for an assignment. Maitefa offered me a choice of two. One, an analysis of the media's portrayal of drugs and youth in the African-American community, and the other an investigation of allegations that slavery still existed in Africa. I chose the latter.

Maitefa made it clear that she did not know whether the allegations were true or false. "Maybe," she said, "it's just a wild story. At the very worst, some one individual or small group may just have been captured and held captive by someone else for a period of time. I don't expect you to go to Africa, Sam. Just research this and see what you can find."

"There is one resource," she added, "a Dr. Charles Jacobs and a Mr. Mohamed Athie. They sent us a press release. Andy saw them on "Tony Brown's Journal" and wants us to look into this. I'll send you the press release, and you can call them.

"Like I said," she repeated, "I don't expect you to go to Africa. Just look into it and do the best that you can."

I returned the receiver to the hook slowly as I thought to myself, "Slavery in Africa...that's crazy! How can that be? This has got to be wrong! I'll look into it, though. Why not? It'll probably be a short piece, and maybe I can also write the piece on drugs and get two stories in."

As I headed back home, walking across Columbia's campus, I was excited about receiving such an interesting and thought-provoking assignment. At the same time, I was experiencing a bit of apprehension. Maitefa had mentioned that this modern-day slavery was possibly occurring in two African countries, Mauritania and Sudan. I had heard of Sudan, but I had never heard of Mauritania. I knew the names of most African nations, but this one just did not ring a bell.

Where in God's name, I wondered, was Mauritania?

◈　　◈　　◈

Then I felt it again. That feeling of apprehension. What was I nervous about? As I walked on, I realized what the problem was: I knew very little about Africa. This article was going to require quite a bit of research.

I shook it off. That wasn't a problem. I was comfortable researching difficult topics. So why was I still feeling so uneasy?

When I thought about it, my doubts were not about whether or not I had the research skills to do the article. No, I was uneasy because I recognized that, although I fancied myself a man proud of my African ancestry, I knew very little about my ancestors' place of origin. I knew even less about contemporary Africans, never having had much interaction with them. Oh, I had a few friends from Africa, like Wisdom Woananu from Ghana and other people I knew from Nigeria, but the truth of the matter was that my associations with them had never sparked in me any real interest in uncovering much beyond the surface of my ancestral past or learning anything about the living children of those ancestors.

I was beginning to doubt myself. I was torn between my doubts and the exciting prospects of researching an issue that was central to everything that

black people had experienced in the United States. I stopped short in the middle of the campus and declared aloud, "You, my brother, are not qualified for this assignment!"

※   ※   ※

I started walking again, heading for the 116th Street station to catch the Number One train to 96th Street, where I would change for a train bound for the Bronx, where I lived. On the train, I asked myself why I had not pursued the study of African history in school, why I knew next to nothing about Africa. Here I was, I thought, ignorant as hell about Africa, yet always making such a fuss about showing my affection for and attraction to what I believed was "African."

I was, to a great extent, a contradiction. I didn't just *look* at Africans, I *watched* them. I *stared* at them. I studied their dark skins and the distinctive facial features that gave them such a regal and exotic air. I entertained a certain pride in Africans; I believed that they were who I would have been had not my forefathers been taken into bondage.

I remembered wishing on many occasions that I, like the Africans from the continent whom I saw and knew, could have a homeland and a language of my own. But I was keenly aware that I was not truly an African, at least not in the same cultural sense that they were. There was a peculiar barrier between me and them, a barrier that I wished did not exist, but one that was real nonetheless. Was it a cultural barrier, or was it something else? I was not sure.

As I crossed the platform to change trains, it came to me why I had never studied African history. I did not really know what to do with all that *knowledge*!

As a kid growing up, when I learned that the great African kingdoms had been corrupted and destroyed, it had simply depressed me. It also angered me that we had once held such an incredibly powerful position in the world and then lost it. I couldn't understand how those great African kings and queens could stand by and let their own people be forced onto the slave ships. How could they watch as the Arabs and the Europeans took us away, beating and humiliating us? That had always bothered me.

As far back as I could remember, the image of slave ships like the Medusa and the Mount Zion had been burned into my consciousness. I could not erase from my mind pictures of my ancestors packed down, scores deep, in those filthy holds, stripped of all their hope and dignity. I connected everything that had happened to black people in this country and around the world to those diabolical vessels criss-crossing the Atlantic with their tragic human cargo.

Mixed with these memories were other recollections equally as painful. I recalled my mother and her friends shaking their heads and sucking their teeth as they sat one day, talking in the living room and passing around a *Jet* magazine. I remembered walking over to my mother and her showing me a picture of a black boy she said had been tortured and murdered in Mississippi.

His name was Emmett Till, she told me, and to this day, I still see his disfigured face as it appeared in that magazine. It didn't look human. It looked like some rag doll that had been torn to pieces. I remembered the photo of the wire Emmett's murderers had placed around his neck and connected to a weight, the weight that was supposed to keep his rag-doll body from surfacing and exposing its watery grave.

I took that *Jet* from my mother and went with it out to the steps in front of our apartment building. I sat down to read it myself, trying to comprehend how someone could beat and torture a little boy to such an extent that he no longer looked human. I stared at the pictures and wondered how afraid Emmett must have been out there in those dark woods with those crazy white men, knowing that no one could hear him scream. I felt anger and helplessness, then and now, because I knew that nothing could be done for him—a little boy so close to my age at the time.

After a long time, I got up and went inside to ask my mother if anything was going to happen to the white men who killed Emmett Till. She said, "Sugar, *nothin'* will be done to those white men! White men can do whatever they want to a nigger, and nothing will happen! Nobody will do anything, least of all not those niggers who live down there in Mississippi! So don't worry about it, baby. Nothing can be done."

Hearing that, I slipped off, as I did many times as a child, into my fantasy world. In my daydreams, I was a warrior, locked away in the putrid hold of a slave ship, waiting for my chance to kill the white men who held me and my people captive. When we saw our chance, I, along with the other warriors, would rise up and fight our way to the deck of the ship. We would kill every white man on board and show them that we too were men who could protect and save our women and children. After we had taken over the ship and turned it around, all the Africans gathered around us would be laughing and crying. We would have a big celebration when we landed back home on the shores of the motherland we thought we would never see again. After the celebration, I would watch as my repatriated companions left to return to their villages, and I would breathe a sigh of relief. Once again, we Africans were safe and sound, and there wasn't going to be any more slavery.

My daydreaming continued until something brought me back to my senses and I realized that Emmett Till was dead, and that I was just another scared little black boy.

A little boy, frightened to death that the white people would do the same thing to me that they did to Emmett when my father and I travelled down lonely southern roads back down to Charlotte, North Carolina, the following summer.

❋   ❋   ❋

Maybe that's why I, and many other African-Americans, don't like thinking about our history—the history of the defeat and destruction of African people is simply too painful—we don't know what to do with it. And then, we can't go back to Africa and boast of the greatness of the kingdoms of Ghana and Songhay in the same way that the English can return to Europe and boast of the British Empire, or Japanese-Americans can return to the Far East and boast of Tokyo's significance in the world.

As I traveled home after receiving my assignment, I realized that I was angry at Africa. And ashamed. Because the history of Africa was too painful to live with, I had alienated myself from it. Yet, on another level, I was also strangely in love with Africa, or with what I thought I knew about her.

Wasn't it me who spent countless hours many weekends picking over and buying authentic African fabrics, garments, multicolored kufis, and vibrant works of art from the Senegalese vendors at the African Market in Harlem. Wasn't it me as well who would drape myself in fashions from the motherland, listen to the powerful rhythms of African music, and feel close, so close, to my confused and tortured ancestral past. How could I feel so proud of this fragile connection to a people and a land I knew almost nothing about?

As the train rumbled out of the 125th Street station, the nagging thought that there were more qualified writers who could really do this story justice again filled my mind. As my car entered the tunnel, I realized at some deeper level that this story could be my doorway to the past. Despite my doubts, I was feeling a growing excitement. As the train resurfaced and the subway car flooded with sunlight, I decided that I, not somebody else, would write the article.

I would just do the best that I could.

Research: The Path to My Past

Maitefa's package containing the press release from the American Anti-Slavery Group arrived a couple of days later. I contacted Jacobs and Athie by telephone and asked them to send whatever additional materials they had directly to me. I asked them if they were sure about their allegations. Jacobs responded that there was plenty of evidence to prove it, and he promised to send me a package of reports and articles right away. No one else had ever written about this issue in depth, he said, and he thanked me and the *City Sun* for having the courage to look into it.

I was a little suspicious and apprehensive about the material Jacobs promised to send me. I expected it to be a strange mixture of odd facts and speculation. Much to my surprise, however, it turned out to be a formidable collection of documents based on sound secondary research. The package was full of articles by other journalists and researchers, reports from the United Nations, interviews from a group called Human Rights Watch/ Africa, entire scholarly journals, and eyewitness testimonies—all recorded and fully documented by reputable and reliable sources. As I examined the material, a horrible picture of contemporary black enslavement, rape, torture, murder, and apartheid began to unfold.

Charles Jacobs had never been to Mauritania or Sudan, but he wasn't spinning or weaving any unfounded theories about slavery in those nations. He had read everything that had been written on the subject, and he was on a mission to bring this atrocious situation to the world's attention. But Jacobs's material was only the beginning of the trail.

◆ ◆ ◆

I began developing my own collection of material by requesting information from sources other than those contained in the package I had been sent. The evidence that I began to receive was absolutely overwhelming. Documents were coming in every day from such sources as the Anti-Slavery Society in London, the U.S. Congress, the Christian Solidarity *International*, *Newsweek International* magazine, the International Labor Office in Geneva, and Amnesty International. I received scores of additional eyewitness reports and newspaper accounts from both Mauritania and Sudan. One of these reports, prepared by Human Rights Watch/Africa, hit me squarely between the eyes. It read:

The institution of slavery continues today in Mauritania, especially in the countryside. Tens of thousands of blacks are considered the property of their masters and are subjected entirely to their master's will. They work long hours for no remuneration. They are denied access to education and do not enjoy the freedom to marry or associate freely with other blacks. They escape servitude, not by exercising their "legal rights," but mainly through escape. Ignorance of their rights, fear of recapture and the torture that often follows, and the lack of marketable skills in an impoverished country discourage a substantial number of slaves from trying to escape.[4]

Tens of thousands of black slaves in Mauritania? The property of Arab-Berber masters? The idea struck me as absolutely incredible! How could this be going on and how could the rest of the world not know?!

As my research continued, it became clear to me that although there was certainly an abundance of data, the world did not know what was happening in northwestern Africa. As I worked my way through the various maps, documents, and articles I had requested and received, a picture of

Mauritania began to emerge in my mind's eye.

◈   ◈   ◈

The country of Mauritania is located in Northwestern Africa. It is bordered by Senegal to the south, Mali to the east, Algeria and the Sahara Desert to the north, and the Atlantic Ocean to the west. It occupies an area of almost 1.1 million square kilometers, thirty percent of which is arid and twenty percent semi-arid.

Mauritania's population, which is estimated at two million people, is one hundred percent Muslim. But that does not stop the practice of abusing and enslaving blacks. There, in that remote corner of Africa, Arabs, free blacks, freed slaves, and slaves are all worshippers of Islam, proving once again that the power of racism supersedes religion.

In the distant past, the land now known as Mauritania was inhabited only by black Africans. Now the rulership of the country is in the hands of Beydanes, literally "white men," of Arab-Berber descent, also known as Moors. What happened to the Africans, and how did Mauritania come to be under the control of these so-called whites? How did slavery and racial oppression come to be a way of life in Mauritania?

The work of Garba Diallo, a Mauritanian scholar, answered many of my questions. According to Diallo, from around the fifth to the twelfth century A.D., the great west African civilizations of Ghana and Tekrur (or Fulani) were flourishing. The ancient kingdom of Ghana had control of the area presently known as Mauritania in the tenth century, but lost it to the invading Almoravids, a Berber dynasty, in the eleventh century. However, Ghana, which evolved into the great empires of Mali and Songhay, would continue to thrive until the seventeenth century. Tekrur later developed into the theocratic kingdom of Fouta Toro.[5]

As these civilizations grew and flourished, storm clouds that would forever change the African landscape were developing and approaching from both the north and the south. The storm clouds on the northern horizon were the migrating Arab tribes, who would defeat and absorb the Berbers. The storm clouds from the south were the French, hell-bent on expanding their colonial reach into western Africa.

It was not simply the lust for conquest that drove the Arabs toward what is now known as Mauritania; it was the twin factors of drought and ecological degradation. In 570 A.D.—forty years before Islam was revealed to the Prophet Mohammed—the Marib Dam near San'a in Yemen collapsed. The ensuing drought spurred several hundred Arab tribes to move northward and eastward into sub-Saharan Africa in search of better grazing land. The most prominent among the Yemenite tribes who engaged in this great migration were the fierce Bani Hilal, who invaded northern Africa around the eighth century. They would reach northern Mauritania by the fourteenth century. Ibn Khaldun, an Arab scholar, described their exodus as follows:

...the Bani Hilal went westward, allegedly destroying, slaying and raping. Like locusts, the Hilalians and their herds (camels) devoured and devastated all forms of vegetable life, reducing the whole area to desert land and creating the severe shortage of timber that later plagued their seafaring descendants.[6]

Directly in the path of this Hilalian firestorm were the nomadic Berbers, the descendants of the pre-Arab populations of northern Africa. The Berbers roamed the northernmost fringes of the Mali and Tekrur empires, from the Egyptian frontier to the Atlantic and from the Mediterranean coast to the Niger. They had no sense of community or ethnic unity beyond their tribal affiliations, which included the Kabyle of Algeria, the Riffians and Shluh of Morocco, and the Tuareg of the Sahara.

A Caucasoid people, the Berbers showed a fairly high incidence of blondness. Their name was derived from a derogatory Greek word for non-Greek, which was later taken into both Latin and Arabic, yielding the English term barbarian. The Berbers called themselves by another name, however: a variant of the word *amazigh*, meaning free man. They spoke variations of a single language, Berber, belonging to the Hamito-Semitic language family.

Although their origins are unknown, the Berbers are thought to have moved into North Africa, probably from the Near East, before 2000 B.C. Beginning about 600 B.C., Berber lands were invaded by various groups, including Carthaginians, Romans, Vandals, and Turks. With the Arab conquest of North Africa in the second half of the seventh century, the Berbers converted to Islam. For awhile they fought alongside the Arabs and helped to extended the frontiers of Islam into Spain. Later, they broke away from both orthodox Islam and Arab hegemony.

Two significant Berber dynasties emerged: the Almoravids (1063-1147 A.D.) and the Almohads (1147-1269 A.D.). Yet, despite the growth of these dynasties, the Berbers never succeeded in ridding themselves of the conquering Arabs.[7] They battled against Arab armies for more than two hundred years until they were finally defeated, in 1644. The Arabs then proceeded to establish four emirates, or town states, in northwestern Mauritania and rapidly Islamified and Arabicized the Berber populations.[8]

These highly mobile Arab-Berber guerrilla forces gradually pushed the stationary and sedentary black Africans of the region further and further south. A long and bloody struggle ensued. Tens of thousands of African men, women, and children were captured and taken into slavery in the north, where they would never again experience freedom. It is their descendants who continue to live in bondage today in Mauritania. Forty percent of that nation's population is presently comprised of current and former slaves. Those who remain enslaved are referred to as *Abid* (singular *Abd*), while those who have been released or who have escaped from slavery are called *Haratines.*[9]

Slavery was common during the time of the Arab-Berber conquests. Indeed, it was or had been practiced by almost every society in the world at that time, including the African society of what we know today as Mauritania. Slavery was an integral part of armed conflict between warring ethnic, tribal, or political groups. When one tribe or group defeated another, it was simply assumed that the victors would take the vanquished as slaves. In the normal sequence of events, newly captured slaves would be traded off and exchanged for slaves who had been captured earlier. In this way, individuals were able to regain their freedom. Others obtained their freedom by finding work and saving enough to purchase freedom for themselves and their family members.

Color was not the most conspicuous criterion for enslavement in what later became Mauritania; however, Garba Diallo makes an important point:

> With the massive influx of Arabs into Mauritania, often under Islamic disguise (many functioning as missionaries) from the eighth century onward, slavery assumed its present black character. From then on, no white-skinned person was ever taken into slavery by the Arabs. This is why one cannot find a single white person among the nearly half a million black slaves who remain in Arab captivity in Mauritania to this day.[10]

It was this region of Africa, with its established system of black chattel slavery, that the French colonized in the 1850s. It is clear that France knew of the existence of slavery in the region because it allowed the colonized Arab-Berbers (or Beydanes, as they are known locally) to "contribute" their black African slaves in lieu of being drafted into military service themselves. Those slaves were later freed, thus explaining why most of the educated Haratines in Mauritania today are the sons and grandsons of slaves who were "given" to the French colonial army in this manner.

By the early 1900s, France was the dominant colonial power in West Africa. The French opted to indirectly govern Mauritania, which was then part of the colony of Senegal, through the existing political structure, which was dominated and controlled by the Beydanes. France subsequently chose to leave the structure of slavery undisturbed, and the colony's blacks remained in bondage. In 1905, France adopted a decree abolishing slavery in the area that later became Mauritania, but no practical measures were ever taken to enforce it.

As in the American South during the post-Civil War era, the abolition of slavery was viewed by both the Arab-Berber elites and the French colonists as a threat to their lives of privilege; thus, they resisted it. When Haratines tried to exercise their freedom and run away, they were captured and returned to their masters by French colonial authorities. Consequently, the emancipation decree was never implemented.[11]

After World War II, France, like several other European nations, was pressured into granting independence to its colonies. However, there was not a great deal of pro-independence activity on either the Arab or the black African side in Mauritania. When the nation of Mauritania was carved out of Senegal and granted its independence in 1960, the former colonial power showed partiality to Arab-Berber rule, despite the Beydanes' history of slaveholding. Thus, in creating this new country, France not only forced two ethnically distinct and historically antagonistic communities—Arab and African—to become one nation, it placed a group that had been holding slaves since 1644 in a position of absolute power.

Soon after independence, the Beydane regime sought to merge the new nation with that of Morocco. The blacks of Mauritania wanted the country to be reunited with Senegal and Mali. This latter push was only natural, given the former colonies' shared history and ancestry. The Senegal River separating the two had never functioned as a real border; people of the same ethnic groups lived and worked on both sides of the river. As the black Mauritanians saw it, the waterway was like a street in the village—the very center of Senegalese society—and traffic moved back and forth across it with ease. During colonial times, many Mauritanian civil servants lived and worked in the colonial capital of St. Louis in Senegal.

Notwithstanding this natural alliance, France, the silent endorser of the chattel enslavement of black Africans in Mauritania, did what all the other European powers had done upon loosening their hold on Africa. It carved up its African territories and, with the stroke of a pen, destroyed connections and relationships that were centuries old. By so doing, in the case of Mauritania, it delivered both free blacks and slaves into the hands of Arab masters.

On November 28, 1960, the independent nation of Mauritania was created. Its first president would be Moktar Ould Daddah, a Beydane, who would abandon the multiparty system and institute one-party rule, effectively eliminating any political power that the nation's black Africans might have aspired to.[12] Since the 1960s, with the help of French colonial and neo-colonial power and influence, the Beydanes have not only continued their culture of slavery but have instituted a system of racial apartheid and subjected Mauritania's black ethnic groups to gross violations of their human rights.

◈   ◈   ◈

As I continued reading through the piles and piles of documents I had received, it became clear to me that the black populations of Mauritania, both slave and free, were living under a violent and deadly system controlled by the Arab-Berber minority. The nation's free Africans, though they have accepted and practice Islam fervently, desired to retain their African culture. They refused to be forced to give up their languages and called themselves "Negro-Africans" to differentiate themselves from the Haratines, who refer to themselves as "black Arabs" and who have lost virtually all aspects of their African culture. I realized as well that the Beydanes were determined to wipe out all manifestations of that culture in Mauritania. Clearly, they had embarked on a program of "Arabization" to strip black Mauritanians of their Africaness and replace it with Arabness.

My resource materials also informed me that there were blacks in Mauritania who were determined to resist such pressures. One of these groups is the Hal-Pulaar. The Hal-Pulaar are the Negro-African ethnic group most resistant to the Beydanes' policy of Arabization. It is they who usually meet with the brunt of the Mauritanian government's oppressive power for their support of the most aggressive political organization protesting the abuses of human rights and the presence of slavery in Mauritania: the African Liberation Forces of Mauritania, or FLAM.

In the early 1980s, FLAM called on the Mauritanian government to take part in a national dialogue to find a peaceful solution to the nation's racial problems through democratic negotiation. This attempt was dismissed by the government as an isolated outburst provoked by a narrow minority of Mauritanian blacks. FLAM responded by publishing a manifesto in April 1986. That manifesto documented, with statistical and other data, that black Mauritanians had been subject to discrimination at all levels of Mauritanian society. The government responded to FLAM's accusations with the arrest of several of the nation's free black intellectuals in September 1986. The jailings were followed by a murderous crackdown on blacks in the Mauritanian army in October 1987.

In December 1987, Negro-Africans protested the execution of three black officers of Hal-Pulaar origin. The government would respond to their protests with more arrests and torture. Amnesty International recorded the testimony of a Negro-African who described an incident that occurred at a police station located, ironically, across the street from the Mauritania Red

Crescent (Red Cross) offices in the capital city of Nouakchott. For three days, this man explained, he was regularly subjected to the "jaguar," a form of torture in which detainees are hung over an iron bar with their hands and feet tied together and then turned on the bar and beaten. He went on to explain the horrors that awaited him and the others:

> *After that, I received electric shocks on the wrists and but-*
> *tocks. They tried to make a hole in the tendon at the back of my*
> *knee with a piece of iron in order to insert an electrode. When*
> *they didn't succeed, they tried with a piece of bone. A few days*
> *later, they tied a weight to my scrotum with string and my testicles*
> *swelled. Then they put hot pepper in my eyes and broke five of my*
> *teeth....For 26 days I urinated only blood. Almost all the detainees*
> *suffered the same fate.*[13]

From August to September 1988, the murder of four prominent black political prisoners would be carried out at Oualata, Mauritania's Devil's Is-land, located in a remote area some twelve hundred kilometers from the cap-ital city of Nouakchott. The nearby village from which the prison, a former French fortress, draws its name was one of the great intellectual and trading centers of the empires of Ghana and Mali from the tenth to fourteenth cen-turies. Oualata today serves as a metaphor for the decline of these once-proud African civilizations and their peoples. For Mauritania's Negro-Africans and Haratines, its mention calls forth a vision of a place where black politi-cal prisoners are barbarously tortured and slain in complete isolation.[14]

Ibrahima Sall, a Negro-African lecturer at the University of Nou-akchott, was one of thirty to forty black intellectuals arrested for publishing an antigovernment proclamation entitled *The Manifesto of the Oppressed Black Mauritanian.* Sall spent ten months at Oualata. In his statement to Human Rights Watch/Africa researchers about his experiences there, he re-lated the following tale of horror:

> *There's nothing worse than hearing cries and knowing you'll*
> *be next. At Oualata, they torture for fifteen, thirty, forty-five min-*
> *utes and you hear terrible screams. Then silence. And you know*
> *someone's next. And then they open the door and take one of us.*[15]

Idrissa Ba, a former livestock specialist with the Ministry of Agriculture who also survived detention at Oualata prison, described a specific incident he and Sall experienced to a Human Rights Watch/Africa investigator:

> *On the evening of March 21, we were all undressed, chained*
> *and hand-cuffed very tightly. We were taken outside in the heat.*
> *They opened our mouths, poured sand into our mouths and*
> *forced us to swallow by pressing our cheeks [and] Brigadier Chief*
> *Mohamed El Habib walked on our heads.*[16]

Oualata prison

Sall continued Ba's harrowing recollection:

...there were about thirty guards in the room. They hit us with batons and iron cords, then made us lie down and hit us on our backs. I felt like a wild animal with others attacking me, shouting "dirty black" and other insults like "you're all Jews" and "we'll kill you all, exterminate you." It was Haratines who beat us....They would also put a foot on your head, with your nose and mouth in the sand, and kick your head. Once the back of my neck was so swollen from this that there was no indent between the back of my head and my shoulders.[17]

"ETHNIC CLEANSING" IN MAURITANIA

An incident that occurred on April 9, 1989, in Diawara, a village on an island in the Senegal River, pushed Mauritania and Senegal to the brink of war and resulted in the death of thousands of Africans. Not only was this a time when Mauritania's relationship with Senegal was in a state of deterioration, but race relations within Mauritania were reaching a critical level. The events that set this terrible period in motion began during the farming season of 1989. Senegalese farmers were prevented from doing what they had done for centuries: they were blocked from cultivating their farms on the Mauritanian side of the Senegal River. Senegal responded by banning Mauritanian camels from grazing on the Senegalese side. A trade embargo followed, and daily confrontations along the border began between blacks and Arabs.

In this atmosphere of conflict, Mauritanian border guards crossed into the Senegalese village of Diawara to fight alongside Mauritanian herders against Senegalese farmers. The guards killed two Senegalese and took thirteen hostages to Selibaby, the provincial capital of the Guidimaka region in the southernmost point of Mauritania. This event sparked anti-Arab demonstrations and the sacking of Arab shops by rioting black youth throughout Senegal. In Mauritania, the killing and hostage-taking unleashed an anti-black massacre. The Arab government used its black slave army to murder over a thousand West African nationals (Senegalese, Ivorians, and Mauritanians) in April 1989. They also deported over two hundred thousand peaceful black citizens to 220 refugee camps in Senegal and Mali.[18]

It was in the city of Nouakchott that much of the Mauritanian violence took place. As one report revealed:

*What began as retaliation against Senegalese ended up being a massacre of anyone who was a black African. Senegalese formed the majority of the deaths, but Malians, Guineans, and Mauritanians—Hal-Pulaars, Wolofs, and Sonin'kes—were also among the scores of those murdered. **Ironically, the main force of the mobs*** *were the black Moors, who struck with such a vengeance—beating, killing, and robbing black Africans.*[19]

Garba Diallo's work indicates that black Africans who were seen as an obstacle to Mauritania's total Arabization were accused of being Senegalese and either hunted down and killed, rounded up and put into detention camps, or deported to Senegal and Mali. Three hundred-fifty villagers were murdered at the Azlat military detention camp in 1990. These brutal acts were merely the tip of the iceberg. Thousands of people were killed during the deportations, their bodies dumped into mass graves such as those discovered later in the village of Sory Male.[20] After the murders, at least 371 villages were destroyed.

Those deported included high-ranking civil servants, army personnel, farmers, and Fulani herdsmen. They were stripped of every-thing, including their clothing and nationality papers, and forced to cross the river to Senegal.[21] Ahmed, a cultivator and shepherd, was expelled from Brakna with four hundred people. He related his story as follows:

> *Three girls drowned. One of them was my twelve-year-old daughter, and the other two were eleven-year-old girls whose families were our neighbors. We were in our village when the gendarmes came, accompanied by Haratines and white Moors armed with guns, axes, and knives. They gathered our belongings and put about fifty or sixty of us—men, women, and children—in a truck. We were searched thoroughly and stripped of our clothes....We were then taken to the river. As there were no boats on the Mauritanian side, we were told to swim. The old people who couldn't swim had to be carried by the men. I had to carry my own father....On June 28, the bodies of the three girls were discovered at different points of the river.*[22]

Women were often subject to sexual harassment during the expulsion process. Several were raped, especially while in detention. Two women from Gnawle gave the following testimony:

> *There was a very old man, seventy-eight, who had his glasses deliberately broken. They made the men cross and brutalized the women. They took a lot of the young women away to be raped and then they brought them back. The women they didn't want, they took off their top clothes. The younger ones were left only in flimsy tops. Then the women and children were driven in trucks to Salinde, about one hundred kilometers away, to board the boats.*[23]

An interview with a Lutheran relief worker who provided aid to Mauritanians deported to Senegal was similarly revealing. Due to fear of reprisals, the worker asked that her identity remain anonymous. She claimed, however, that African women had been attacked in Mauritania, that their earrings had been torn out, and that large chunks of flesh had been cut out of their breasts.[24]

Due to the shame Mauritanian Muslims typically associate with sexual abuses, Human Rights Watch/Africa was not able to gather much testimony from the victims of such attacks. A former employee of the U.S. embassy described the last stages of the treatment of a group of detainees before they were expelled:

> They took us to a cereal warehouse and made us sit down in a filthy corner for five hours....There was a customs officer who terrorized everyone; he was especially hard on the women. The women were searched with a vindictiveness that was shameful, including their private parts. Several women were raped.[25]

From November 1990 through February 1991, five thousand black Mauritanian service and civil servants were arrested and detained for several months without being charged. After they were released, it was discovered that five to six hundred of them had been executed or tortured to death by government forces. Human Rights Watch/Africa confirmed that these detainees were subjected to a savage cruelty that almost defies description. Particularly egregious was the fact that many who survived were reportedly crippled, paralyzed, or maimed from torture. Many others were believed to have died from their wounds after their release.[26]

Human Rights Watch/Africa identified the following methods of torture used by the Beydanes against their black Mauritanian countrymen: beatings all over the prisoners' bodies using fists, boots, sticks, rubber tubing, electrical cords, and/or rifle butts; stripping the prisoners naked and pouring cold water over them (especially when if they arrived in December, when it was cold); burying prisoners in sand up to their necks and then pulling their hair out, burning their faces with lit cigarettes; and burning, electric shock, and beating of prisoners' genitals (both males and females). There were also reports of castrations, allegedly performed to curtail what Beydane extremists referred to as black Mauritanians' "uncontrollable" fertility.[27] According to a U.S. State Department report, some of the detainees at the infamous Inal prison in northern Mauritania "were tied by their testicles to the rear of a four-wheel-drive vehicles and dragged at high speeds through the desert."[28] This document further maintains that "several [men]...including a Captain Lome Abdoulaye, a former senior officer in the Mauritanian navy, died as a result of this particular treatment."[29]

A black Mauritanian chief warrant officer shared his account of the inhumane treatment suffered by Negro-Africans sent to Inal in an interview with representatives from Human Rights Watch/Africa. One of few survivors, the officer said that he was arrested on November 27, 1990, and told only that he was being sent to Inal, a small village that serves as a whistle stop for trains running from Zouerate to Nouad-hibou carrying iron ore. However, he soon learned that he and several others captured with him were not bound for the village of Inal; they were headed for the military base of the same name located near the village. At the time, the base was considered the worst place a Mauritanian political prisoner could be sent.

Inal was a place of extermination. People were sent there to be murdered. Of the five to six hundred persons believed to have been tortured to death by government forces during this period of ethnic cleansing, two hundred would be killed at Inal alone. According to the officer:

At 9 A.M., the captain of the base of Inal came with two groups of six people, each with a whip. They began to beat us, and did so from 9 to 11:30 A.M. Afterwards they took us to a warehouse where we found friends of ours who were almost dead, people who couldn't even talk. The place was stinking, as if there were only dead bodies there. They then tied us with chains which were there and beat us every hour and insulted us, dirty words. They said we are savages who shouldn't have existed, that we are people who cannot be in Mauritania...that they were going to kill all the adults and only the children would be left, and these children would be taught Hassaniya or Arabic. French, Hal-Pulaar, Sonin'ke, and Wolof would no longer exist in Mauritania.

They kept on torturing us until around 7:00 P.M. The first person I saw hanged in front of my eyes was a soldier called Idi Seck. They took the rope, put it around his neck and tied him. They left him till he died....Afterwards, around midnight, they brought ropes, made three rows of ten people each and hanged thirty people. It was on the occasion of the feast of November 28 [Independence Day].[30]

In December 1992, the Arab-Berber officers directly responsible for the killings were identified by the survivors, but the Mauritanian government refused to allow any legal action to be taken against them. Instead, it gave the accused officers scholarships to attend France's military academy, located near Paris, and promptly sent them overseas. On May 29, 1993, President Maaouya Ould Sid Ahmed Taya ordered his Parliament to pass an amnesty law exonerating any member of the security forces who might have violated human rights between 1989 and 1992.[31]

Thus began the final stage of the Beydane's ethnic cleansing program. Soon thereafter, the Mauritanian government launched an effort to confiscate free black Mauritanians' citizenship papers, businesses, land, and cattle; and it began to drive these Negro-Africans out of the country and across the Senegal River into Senegal. To add to the Africans' humiliation, their expropriated farms were given to Beydane businessmen and to Palestinian and Malian Tuareg immigrants.[32]

The act of giving black Mauritanians' land to the Tuaregs is further indicative of the Mauritanian government's position on race and slavery. Tuaregs are the Berber-speaking people who for centuries controlled the valuable trans-Saharan caravan trade in slaves, gold, and ivory.[33] They, too, continue to practice slavery to this day. Many brought their slaves with them to Mauritania, as documented by United Nations observers' reports of the Malian refugees, both Tuareg and Maur, who arrived in the camps established for them in the eastern part of the country by the Mauritanian government. According to these informed sources, an estimated ten percent of the eighty thousand refugees in these refugee camps were slaves. Reportedly, "Efforts by U.N. workers in the camps to distribute food and other services to these families separately from their masters [met] with strong resistance by the slaves themselves, who [may have feared] retribution from their masters."[34]

I found this last bit of information even more shocking. Slaves brought into Mauritania from Mali? Did this mean that black Africans were being held as slaves in Mauritania, Sudan, and Mali? Three nations, instead of two? Were there more?

◈   ◈   ◈

By the time I finished this portion of my research, I was literally overwhelmed by the documented suffering of the so-called "free" blacks of Mauritania. And I had yet to investigate thoroughly any claims about the existence of a slave society in that nation.

I began drafting my article, first outlining the following information in tabular form to help me and my potential readers better understand the structure of Mauritanian society. Breaking things down in this way revealed the presence of four groups rather than the two or three mentioned in most of the official literature. In those texts, Mauritania's ethnic groups are usually described as consisting of only the Moors and the Negro-Africans, or of just the white Moors, black Moors, and Negro-Africans. There was clearly evidence of a resistance on the part of demographers to address the existence of the fourth group: Mauritania's slave population.

It was now my responsibility to address this group's existence, to read and try to understand the wretchedness of their lives, and to reveal it to the world. After learning of all the horrors faced by the Negro-Africans of Mauritania, I was deeply disturbed. Based on their stories alone, whatever fantasies I had entertained of Africa prior to undertaking my research were quickly dissolving. I felt as if I was going to choke from the humiliation I felt them suffering in large quantities. I was beginning to feel boxed in by oppressive darkness. I had a strong desire to push all of my background materials away and turn the light back on in my life, to breathe again.

I sensed that I was descending into a place that was not healthy. I prayed silently that I could handle all that awaited me.

MAURITANIA'S SOCIAL STRUCTURE
ETHNIC GROUPS

Arab-Berbers/Moors/Beydanes

These Mauritanians typically refer to themselves as <u>Arabs</u>. The government of Mauritania, which they dominate, does not even admit the existence of Berbers in the country. As such, the newly introduced constitution of the country stipulates: "The people of Mauritania are Muslim, Arab and African."[35] The Beydanes (meaning "white" in Arabic), as they are locally known, are nevertheless a mixture of Arab, Berber, and African stock who have become united by language and religion. They speak an Arabic/Berber dialect called Hassaniya.

The name "Moor" is surrounded by controversy and has a number of meanings. One explanation is that it comes from the Latin word "Mauri," the name for the Berber inhabitants of the old Roman province of Mauretania, the territory now covered by Morocco and part of Algeria. In a general sense, it refers to people of mixed ancestry who live in North Africa. It is also used to identify a member of the Muslim populations of North Africa. This latter designation includes the Arab and Arabicized Berbers who conquered Spain and established Muslim rule in the Iberian peninsula from the eighth to the seventeenth century A.D. However, some black scholars of African history have a different view. Edward Scobie, for instance, contends that all of the Moors were Africoid in origin, citing Chancellor Williams, who maintains that:

> *The original Moors, like the original Egyptians, were black Africans. As amalgamation became more and more widespread, only the Berbers, Arabs and coloureds in the Moroccan territories were called Moors, while the darkest and black skinned Africans were called 'Black-a-Moors.' Eventually, 'black' was dropped from 'Blackamoor.' In North Africa, and Morocco in particular, all Muslim Arabs, mixed breeds and Berbers are readily regarded as Moors. The African Blacks, having had even this name taken from them, must contend for recognition as Moors."*[36]

In Mauritania, the term "Moor" is used to identify the Arab-Berber and the people of African descent who have been freed from slavery—that is, the Haratines. There is no desire on the part of Negro-Africans to be identified as Moors.

Chattel Slaves

The enslavement of black Africans has been practiced in Mauritania for many centuries. Black Africans were kidnapped into slavery by Arab Mauritanians as early as 1644, and their successive generations have never been emancipated. It is estimated that tens of thousands of black Africans live in chattel slavery in Mauritania today and are being used for labor, for their masters' sexual gratification, and for breeding. As a result of their degradation, these enslaved Africans (called "*Abid*," or "*Abd*" in the singular form) have lost almost every aspect of their Africaness except their black skin color.

Haratines, or Freed Slaves

The Haratines are people of Negroid descent who were kidnapped and forced into slavery by the Mauritanian Arabs. The term "Haratine" is derived from the Arabic word for "freedom," yet these people are believed by the Negro-Africans (non-slaves) to be the wretched of the desert. In Mauritania, the term has been applied to former slaves who, like the Abid, remain economically and culturally attached to their present or former Arab masters to this day. Like the chattel slaves, the Haratines too have lost virtually every aspect of their African origins except their skin color.

Negro-Africans

Non-slave black ethnic groups in Mauritania use this term to distinguish themselves from the Haratines. Although these people are engaged in a struggle to resist Arabization and retain their African culture, traditions, and language, they fervently worship Islam. Mauritania's Negro-Africans are comprised of the following groups in order of size:

The *Fulani* are called by different names such as Fulbe, Fulata, Fulah, Fulani, Hal-Pulaar, Peul, and Toucoulor, depending on where they live. They speak Pulaar (or Fulfulde) and generally refer to themselves as Fulbe (singular: Pullo). They are primarily farmers and herdsmen and inhabit the savanna belt stretching from the Sudan to Mauritania.

The *Sonin'ke* are the indigenous people of Mauritania. They are the descendants of the founders of the kingdom of Ghana, which occupied the land that presently comprises southeastern Mauritania in the early fifth century A.D. Today, the Sonin'ke are mainly concentrated in that region's Guidimakha, Assaba, and Hodh territories. They are also found in western Mali, northeastern Senegal, and in Gambia. The Sonin'ke belong to the Mande ethnic group. Their main economic activities are agriculture and trade.

The *Wolof* are mainly concentrated in the Rosso (Trarza) region of Mauritania, which abuts the southwestern border of Senegal, and in the urban centers of Senegal and Gambia. They generally earn their living as fishermen, farmers, and traders.

The *Bambara* number perhaps no more than ten thousand individuals. They live mainly in the eastern part of the nation, in the village of Kankosa and in cities such as Nema and Aiouen. The largest concentration of Bambara is in Mali and eastern Senegal. Like the Sonin'ke and the Wolof, they are part of the great Mande people.[37]

The *Imraguen* are the smallest Negro-African group still held in Arab bondage in Mauritania. They number no more than a couple of hundred persons, and few people, including most Mauritanians, know much about them. Reportedly, "they are vassals to the Hassan (Arab) tribes, particularly of the Awlad Bou Sba. They live in dismal huts and live off fishing in the region stretching from Cape Timiris to Nouadhibou."[38] They speak a distinctively different language from that of other Negro-African groups.

CHAPTER TWO

A person born a slave is always a slave unless freed. Children are the property of masters; slave parents have no rights to their children. The slave is the property of the master and so are the slave's off spring in perpetuity. The slave is brought up with the master's family and begins work as soon as possible. Of course, the masters abuse the slaves, both sexually and in terms of work. Slavery goes through the woman, so that if a master impregnates a slave girl, the children belong to him. Sometimes a master may fall in love with his slave and marry her; when she marries a master, she is automatically freed.[1]
—MOHAMMED SALLEK, Mauritania

SLAVERY AND THE ANTI-SLAVERY MOVEMENT IN MAURITANIA

As I read the history of slavery in Mauritania, I realized that it was the story of a country with an unbroken tradition of enslaving black people. The Mauritanian reality was diametrically opposed to the widespread modern belief that the buying and selling of human beings had ceased with the advent of the twentieth century. Indeed, this African nation seemed unaffected by the passage of time or by any of the events relative to the abolition of slavery that had transpired in the past one hundred years.

Think about it: As recently as July 5, 1980, Mauritanian President Mohamed Khouna Ould Haidallah issued a decree abolishing slavery in his country, thus marking the fourth time leaders of this tiny nation had seen fit to do so. Prior to the 1980 decree, slavery had been outlawed in 1901, 1905, and again in 1961. The first of these woefully ineffective mandates was issued by the French colonial government on February 1, 1901. It stated that a master no longer had the right to pursue and recover a slave who had escaped from slavery. The December 12, 1905, decree established fines for persons who entered any agreements that resulted in the enslavement of another individual. Like its predecessor, this ruling effected little if any change.

The third decree, issued on May 20, 1961, as Article 1 of the Constitution of Mauritania, declared that the new republic assured equality before the law to all its citizens without distinction of race, religion or social condition. This, statement, however, was interpreted by the Beydane ruling class as simply a token, indirect abolition of slavery—a fanciful facade to assuage Western sensibilities. If it had been carried out, they reasoned, it would have meant that former slaves, despite their abject social condition, would henceforth have held all of the rights previously denied to them. Of course, such an article was ridiculous to the Beydanes. It was subsequently never enforced, and slavery continued to exist.[2]

Like the three decrees preceding it, President Haidallah's 1980 decree was also meaningless. This became crystal clear in the following year when the ruling Military Committee of National Salvation adopted Ordinance Number 81.234 on November 9, 1981. A close examination of this ordinance reveals that it was actually a means of ensuring the continuation of slavery in Mauritania. As it states:

> After the Military Committee of National Salvation's deliberation and adaptation, the President of the Committee promulgates the ordinance:

> **First Article:** Slavery in all its forms is definitively abolished throughout the territory of the Islamic Republic of Mauritania.

> **Second Article:** In keeping with the Shari'a [Islamic] law, this abolition will imply a payment of compensation to those entitled to such...

> **Third Article:** A national commission, composed of Ulama [Islamic religious leaders], economists, and administrators will be instituted by decree to study the modalities of this compensation. These modalities will be fixed by decree once the study is finished.

> **Fourth Article:** This ordinance will be published without delay and implemented as law.[3]

Like the three anti-slavery mandates issued before it, Ordinance Number 81.234 abolished slavery throughout the land. It is important to note, however, that the 1981 ordinance made no mention of the need for the government to institute programs to facilitate the freeing of slaves. Nor does it say anything about the allocation of resources to address the former slaves' subsequent needs for food, clothing, and shelter. No mention is made of provisions for the former slaves' education or other social mechanisms that might speed their re-entry into Mauritanian society. The ordinance does not call for the creation of law enforcement bodies that slaves can turn to for assistance or redress, nor does it stipulate any punishment for those who continue to engage in slavery. And there is certainly no mention of moral or material compensation for the freed slaves. In fact, the opposite holds true. This article addresses only the compensation due to slaveholders.[4]

Embodied in a decree that on the surface eliminates slavery in Mauritania, articles two and three actually perpetuate the enslavement of black Mauritanians. Article Two calls for the imposition of Islamic Shari'a laws insofar as compensation is concerned, yet it is purposely vague. As a result, the Mauritanian legal system commonly assumes that this article refers to compensation by the slave to his or her former master, and not by the master to his or her former slave. This stacks the deck almost impossibly against the ex-slave since few possess any goods of much value and most former masters demand substantial compensation for their loss of valuable property.

Article Three ensures that even if a former slave is able to obtain a hearing in court, his or her chances for freedom will be slim, indeed. It places the decision authority for determining the amount of "fair" compensation in the hands of Islamic religious leaders or Ulama, the majority of whom, in Mauritania are Arabs. Subsequently, under the jurisdiction of the Ulama, the courts almost always decide in favor of the master. As a 1992 *Newsweek International* report confirmed:

> *The Mauritanian government never passed any laws providing punishment for enslaving black Africans and they never bothered to tell many of the slaves about emancipation. In 1980, the government sought to have its ruling ratified by a body of religious jurists, the ulama. The jurists said that slavery is not wrong on religious grounds, but that outlawing it would be within the government's competence—provided that owners were compensated for the manumission of slaves. Nobody has ever applied for compensation.[5]*

A 1994 Human Rights Watch/Africa report corroborated the *Newsweek* study. That report held that religion, specifically Islam, was being used by Mauritania's Beydanes "as an important instrument to perpetuate slavery."[6] The report continued:

> *Relying on the fact that Islam recognizes the practice of slavery, [Beydane slaveholders] have misinterpreted it to justify current practices. In truth, Islam only permits treating as slaves*

non-Islamic captives caught after holy wars, on condition that
they be released as soon as they convert to Islam. People living
as slaves in Mauritania long before the first abolition in 1905
were Muslims, but this did not lead to their emancipation. We
received numerous complaints about the extent of which qadis
[judges in Islamic courts] continue to exercise their judicial
functions to protect the institution of slavery, rather than to en-
sure its eradication.[7]

Likewise revealing are the comments of Mauritanian anti-slavery leader
Boubacar Messaoud:

As long as the masters are not compensated, they do not need
to free any slaves. Faced with the lack of legislation, the modern
law courts proclaim they have no jurisdiction in the matter and ei-
ther dismiss cases submitted to them or refer them to the Islamic
law courts. Although they are civil servants, the judges in the Is-
lamic courts almost always rule in favor of the masters, hiding be-
hind tradition to justify the confiscation of property and the
confinement of people against their will, in particular women and
children, who are easier to control and are often passed off as
wives or children of the master.[8]

In support of his claims, Messaoud cited as evidence two recent cases.
The first was the case of Zeid El Mal and his wife Bilal, their daughter
M'Barka, and their son S'Haba, which came before the Islamic court in the
town of Aleg in the region of Brakna. In its ruling of February 7, 1996, the
court took the two children away from their parents and returned them to
their master, Ahmed Ould Nacer, a Beydane of the Arouejatt tribe. Although the parents lodged appeals immediately after the ruling, judgment in
the case is still pending.

Another example described by Messaoud reportedly took place in 1994
in Barkéol, a city in Mauritania's Assaba region. There, farmer Mohamed
Ould Bilal, son of a slave, had his field expropriated upon his father's death
by the heir of his father's owners. The matter was later referred to the
mixed chamber of the Mauritanian Supreme Court, which upheld the pre-
vious judgment in 1995. Three appeals later, to three successive ministers of
justice, Mohamed Ould Bilal is still waiting for the courts to respond.[9]

Thus, Ordinance 81.234, while similarly as ineffective as the preceding
proclamations in abolishing slavery, was significantly different. More than a
public relations ploy, it was actually a means of fortifying and ensuring the
continuation of slavery in Mauritania. Yet, beyond laying to rest Beydane
fears of the end of their slave-holding privilege, what was the reason behind
this meaningless ordinance? It was actually part of a plan to rob credit for

Boubocar Messaoud

the emancipation initiative away from a Haratine anti-slavery group called El Hor ("The Free").

El Hor is one of two organizations not recognized by the Mauritanian government that has long been active in protesting the existence of chattel slavery in Mauritania. It came into existence in 1974 with an agenda to raise the consciousness of the nation's Abid and Haratine communities. Its members maintain that without strong measures to enforce anti-slavery laws and adequate provisions to provide former slaves with the means to gain economic independence through programs such as agricultural cooperatives, there can be no real emancipation of Mauritania's enslaved populations.

The other unrecognized anti-slavery activist group is called SOS-Esclaves. Under the leadership of its president, Boubacar Messaoud, SOS-Esclaves' mission is to assist the Abid in their struggle for emancipation and in regaining custody of children who have been sold or kidnapped. It also carries out human rights awareness campaigns among those still enslaved to educate them about their rights. Despite its work, or perhaps because of it, the Mauritanian government refuses to recognize SOS-Esclaves.[10]

An incident that took place in February 1980 brought El Hor into direct confrontation with the government. That incident involved the sale of the slave woman named Mbarka in Atar, a city in northwestern Mauritania. Atar is one of the most important and strategic population centers in Mauritania and the administrative capital of the Adar region. In this key city, one month after President Haidallah came to power as the result of a military coup, El Hor came into direct confrontation with the government.

It happened that Mbarka was very beautiful, and her master believed he could get a very good price for her on the open market. The sale itself was nothing out of the ordinary in Mauritania, but a dispute arose between an educated Haratine, Lieutenant Barak Ould Barek, who wanted to marry Mbarka, and two Beydanes who wanted to buy her. The fate of the woman came to national attention, and El Hor used the incident as a vehicle to address broader issues of slavery and freedom in Mauritania.

The group quickly organized anti-slavery demonstrations in a number of areas, including the towns of Nouakchott, Rosso, and Nouadhibou. The government responded with oppression, and several El Hor leaders were arrested, severely tortured, and exiled. Undaunted, the organization continued its activities underground.

President Haidallah immediately took steps to undermine the swelling anti-slavery movement's power.[11] Chief among the government's tactics were efforts aimed at co-opting some of the movement's spokesmen. Select members of El Hor were given government posts, promotions, and economic opportunities.[12]

The government also issued its toothless anti-slavery decree in 1980.

Despite these efforts, the anti-slavery movement continued to gain momentum throughout the country. The new regime became very concerned about possible linkages between El Hor and Negro-African opposition groups. Thus, on November 9, 1981, President Haidallah issued Ordinance Number 81.234.

❖　❖　❖

Instead of attacking slavery and putting pressure on those who practiced it, the Beydane government's strategy was to direct the eyes of the world away from the issue. They did this by creating a special nongovernmental organization (NGO) called the Comité de Lutte pour L'Eradication des Se'quelles de L'Esclavage en Mauritanie (the Committee for the Eradication of the Vestiges of Slavery In Mauritania). The goal of this organization was to put a favorable spin on the deplorable status of human rights attainment in that nation—to lead the international human rights community to believe that slavery no longer exists in Mauritania and that only the vestiges of slavery remain.

Neither the Committee nor any Mauritanian governmental authorities have developed any economic, social, or education programs to aid the slaves who were purportedly freed by the 1901, 1905, 1961, 1980, and 1981 edicts.[13] They have never even initiated an awareness campaign to inform those blacks who remain enslaved about the existence of any emancipation ordinances. Local authorities, specifically the *hakem* (prefects of provinces) and the wali (governors of regions), refuse to receive and register complaints from slaves. According to Boubacar Messaoud, "This attitude amounts to a form of complicity with the slave-owners, since a 'non-existent' problem cannot be solved, just as an imaginary illness cannot be treated."[14]

After a fact-finding mission to Mauritania in 1982, a study group commissioned by the London-based Anti-Slavery Society estimated that at least a hundred thousand full-time slaves and more than three hundred thousand semi-slaves remained in bondage there, the "property" of Mauritanian-Beydane slaveholders.[15] Four years after President Haidallah's 1980 edict, a UN mission confirmed the total absence of any concrete measures by Mauritanian authorities in favor of the slaves.[16] As Newsweek's 1992 report of a year-long study of Mauritanian slavery concluded:

> *More than 100,000 descendants of Africans conquered by Arabs during the twelfth century are still thought to be living as old-fashioned chattel slaves in Mauritania....Aside from the shantytowns and a strip of land along the Senegal River, virtually all blacks are slaves, and they are more than half the population.*[17]

THE LIFE OF A SLAVE

As recently as 1994, a Human Rights Watch/Africa report attested that Mauritania's black African slaves were being subjected to all of the mental and emotional torments that are typically associated with slavery. According to that report:

> Routine punishments [of slaves] for the slightest fault include beatings, denial of food and prolonged exposure to the sun, with hands and feet tied together. However, serious violations of the master's law, such as disobeying orders, attempting to escape or even the mere suspicion of wanting to escape, being in contact with free blacks, inciting other slaves to escape, and having sexual relations with [a member of] the master's family bring severe and macabre torture down on the head of the disobedient slave. The severity of the torture is not only to serve as an example to others, but to insure [sic] that the slave becomes incapable of enjoying normal sexual relations with women. Women are spared [these] types of torture because the primary value of the female slave is her reproductive capacity.[18]

The report further maintains that serious infringements of "the master's law" can result in a slave becoming the recipient of prolonged and vicious forms of torture. One such torture, called the "camel treatment," is administered to male slaves only. The man is strapped atop a camel that has deliberately been denied water for up to two weeks; his ankles are tied together under the camel's belly. The camel is then allowed to drink, and as its stomach expands, the slave's legs, thighs, and groin are slowly distended and eventually dislocated. Slaves punished in this way are left tied to the camel for up to four or five days and subsequently not given any medical treatment.

A man named Moustapha related the following incident to a Human Rights Watch/Africa investigator:

> A slave I know suffered the camel treatment in 1988 in Sharat, west of Boghe'. His master suspected him of wanting to escape, because they found him on the road when he should not have been there. In addition, he was an outspoken young man who tended to reply back to the master and his family and made it clear that he did not like the life of a slave. He was recaptured and put through the camel method. He was 16 at the time. He is still living with the master's family but is so handicapped that he is not capable of performing any tasks.[19]

Moustapha, the former slave mentioned previously, described another torture called the "insect treatment." As he explained it, tiny insects are stuffed into the ears of the victim and small stones are used to ensure that the insects remain inside them. A scarf is then tied tightly around the victim's head, and his or her hands and feet are also tied to prevent movement. The scarf and stones are removed after several days, by which time the victim's mind is typically destroyed.

Moustapha recalled an incidence of this particularly devious form of torture that occurred in 1986 when the slave, Mohamed Ould Barek, left his master's home to visit a neighboring Hal-Pulaar village and was absent for a day or two longer than anticipated. His master went to look for him, fearing that he had escaped. When Barek was found, his master tied a rope around his neck, attached the rope to his camel, and dragged him along on the road as he rode home. Upon returning, Barek was immediately subjected him to the insect treatment, which, according to Moustapha, drove him insane.[20]

There is also the "burning coals" torture, again typically administered to males, wherein the offender is seated on the ground with his legs spread apart. Hot coals are placed between his thighs, and he is buried in sand up to his waist to prevent him from moving. After awhile, the thighs, legs, and sex organs of the victim are burned.

Slaves caught fleeing are often castrated or branded like cattle upon their return to their masters. One black Mauritanian health worker in Atar described the brutal treatment meted out to a slave youth who had been caught sleeping with his master's daughter:

> *The boy, who was seventeen, had a piece of wire tied tightly around his genitals and the wire was in turn attached, for two days, to a rope. He was beaten and water poured all over him. I saw him myself. He had become so handicapped that the master could not use him at all; so he "emancipated" him.*[21]

There are other gruesome tortures, states the Human Rights Watch/ Africa report.[22] From almost all of these interviews, however, a consistent and ominously violent pattern of slave life and human degradation emerges. References to efforts and activities whose goal is to reduce slaves to the level of animals are frequent.

One article that I read as part of my background research featured an interview, conducted by Jesse Washington of the Associated Press and published in Vibe magazine, with Mauritanian refugee and former UNESCO worker El Hadj Demba Ba. As Demba Ba explained:

> *These people [Arab-Berbers], who consider slaves to be a sign of wealth, often live in tents with all the different families of a clan pitching their tents together to form villages. At the side of each tent is a branch-roof pen that serves as home to animal and*

abd, the Arabic word for "slave." The master usually mixes the slaves with the animals. Donkeys, sheep, cows, camels—you [the slave] are the one to take care of them. You even eat with them, drink with them, live with them, and sleep with them. So, what do you become? You become an animal.[23]

This concept of the bestialization of slaves was examined more broadly in another article I received: David Brion Davis's "At the Heart of Slavery," published in the *New York Times Review of Books*. According to Davis:

Though historians have long recognized dehumanization as central to slavery, they have not—despite the significant clue Aristotle provided when he called the ox "the poor man's slave"—explored its bestializing aspects. This neglected point seems to me central. Drawing on comparisons of slaves with domestic animals that have been made throughout history, Karl Jacoby has argued convincingly that the domestication of sheep, goats, pigs, cattle, horses, and other animals during the Neolithic revolution served as a model for enslaving humans.

[W]hether used for food, clothing, transport, or heavy labor, these domesticated animals underwent an evolutionary process of neotony, or progressive "juvenilization." That is, they became more submissive than their wild counterparts, less fearful of strangers, and less aggressive....Despite the many attempts to equate human captives with domestic animals—the first African slaves shipped to Lisbon in the mid-1400s were stripped naked and marketed and priced exactly like livestock—slaves have fortunately never been held long enough in distinct, isolated groups to undergo significant hereditary change. Yet neotony, the development of childlike characteristics in slaves, was clearly the goal of many slaveholders, despite their lack of any scientific understanding of how domestication had changed the nature and behavior of animals...[24]

Over and over again, the interviews I read, those of Mauritanian free blacks and former slaves as well as other observers, made it clear that not only has a process of dehumanization been going on in this part of Africa for centuries, but the process of bestialization or neotony has also been successfully accomplished.

Demba Ba's comments also described the psychological effects of chattel slavery on Mauritanian blacks:

When you become friendly with freed Haratines, they treat you just like their superior. They come to your house and want to do the dirty jobs. You have to remind them: "You sleep with me, you eat with me, whatever we do, we do it together." But some of *them refuse it, and you end up hating them. I talked to those who are in the deepness of slavery, I tell them, "You can work for your own self and be free, like me." They say, "I don't think I can make it without my master. My master gives me food, the clothes I am wearing. What else can I do? I've never been to school. I don't own any property. Where am I going to live if I run away?"*[25]

The observations of longtime Mauritanian resident Father François Lefort provided additional valuable insights into the psychological power Mauritanian Beydanes wield over their black African slaves:

> *The slave lives in perpetual awe of his masters and is not aware of any other way of life. He would often be utterly shocked if he saw his master work or carry a burden. The bond between slave and master is very strong and in many cases, a Haratine would spontaneously continue to help and support his former master and would even "lend" him his daughters and sons to work as servants or shepherds. Slaves never complain and even those who have escaped do not bear grudges against their former masters except when they have been subjected to violence or abuse.*[26]

These first-hand descriptions corroborate the findings of Orlando Patterson, who points out in his recent work, Slavery and Social Death, that "an ideological imperative of all systems of slavery" is the total eradication of "any hint of 'manhood'" among slaves.[27] Patterson quotes historian Stanley Elkins's infamous description of the stereotypical slave such systems consider the "ideal" product:

> *Sambo, the typical plantation slave, was docile but irresponsible, loyal but lazy, humble but chronically given to lying and stealing; his behavior was full of infantile silliness and talk inflated with childish exaggeration. His relationship with his master was one of utter dependence and childlike attachment: it was indeed this childlike quality that was the very key to his being.*[28]

As David Brion Davis explains:

> *This stereotype describes precisely what a human male slave would be like if slaves had been subjected to the same process as that of domesticated animals....While ancient Greeks saw such slave-like traits in the people they called "barbarians" and the stereotype was much later associated with so-called Slavs—the root of the word "slave" in Western European languages—it was only in the fifteenth century, when slavery increasingly became linked with various peoples from sub-Saharan Africa, that the stereotype began to acquire specific racial connotations. As slav-*

ery in the Western world became more and more restricted to Africans, the arbitrarily defined black "race" took on all the qualities, in the eyes of many white people, of the infantilized and animalized slave.[29]

As Demba Ba and the others maintain, the psychological control of Mauritanian slaveholders over their slaves and former slaves after four centuries of servitude is profound. The Human Rights Watch/Africa testimony of an elderly Mauritanian woman who was formerly a slave further illuminates this:

We hear of abolition, but for most slaves it does not mean much. It is hard to ignore what they have been told all their lives, that without their master they cannot survive, that only he can ennoble them, give meaning to their life and lead them to heaven. They believe this; so how can they also believe that they must escape the situation that promises to give them so much?[30]

This woman's comments also touch upon an aspect of control that cannot be ignored when discussing the issue of slavery in Mauritania: the power of religion and how it is manipulated by Beydane slaveholders to justify and bolster their position of dominance over the nation's blacks.

◈　◈　◈

In Mauritania, slaves are raised by their masters to believe that serving their masters is their religious duty. They are subsequently exposed to a false teaching of Islam that justifies their enslavement, even though the slaves are themselves Muslims. Mauritanian slaves are taught to accept their subordinate position as a condition for going to heaven. Indeed, a popular saying among them is that "the way to heaven is underneath the sole of your master's foot." According to a Mauritanian religious leader from Aleg:

It is difficult for a slave to go to the mosque to pray because they have not been taught what to recite. After the last abolition [1980], the masters intimidated their slaves by telling them that their choice was to follow them or to go to hell. Given the culture they had lived in all their lives, it is easy to understand why so many believe this.[31]

Another of the nation's black African religious leaders had this to say:

I never had a slave as a student in Koranic school. They are not permitted to attend. I only had as pupils a few whose parents had escaped to the city; otherwise, no slaves came as students. Once at school, if they are regarded as having developed a "disrespectful" attitude, they are sent to the countryside to tend the animals.[32]

The government of Mauritania also deepens the divisions between free blacks and slaves by using Haratines and slaves to control and suppress the Negro-Africans. For example, in February 1966, armed Haratines were employed to stop free black students from rioting in Nouakchott. In April 1989, Abid and Haratines who lived in the countryside and who had the least contact with other blacks, played a key role in the ethnic cleansing of over one hundred thousand of Mauritania's Negro-African citizens.[33]

One result of what has been a long history of both covert and overt divisive tactics is that Abid and Haratines presently share only black skin in common with the Negro-African ethnic groups of Mauritania. Abid and Haratine Mauritanians consider themselves Arabs and speak Arabic, while the free blacks call themselves Negro-Africans and speak French. Other distinctions make it easy to recognize who among Mauritania's black populations is a slave and who is not. The Abid and Haratines wear robes and head scarves of plain colors in the Arab style; the free Africans typically dress in traditional African garb and vivid prints, and regard their enslaved or former slave countrymen with a mixture of disgust and pity.

SLAVERY ON BOTH SIDES OF THE RIVER

As additional background research, I interviewed several Mauritanians who were living in New York. These expatriates confirmed for me something that I had read in African scholar Garba Diallo's book of interviews and photographs of slaves in northwestern Africa: that Beydane masters often transported their slaves across the Senegal River to work in the boutiques and stores of Dakar and as domestic servants. One of the slaves Diallo interviewed was named Abdi. What follows is Diallo's narrative:

What I want to tell you about is now, [in] 1995. It is the story about a black Mauritanian slave whose name is Abdi. Abdi is not an ordinary name which free people choose for their children. Abdi means "slave" in Arabic and the name is typically reserved for black slaves....

Because of the massive sexual exploitation of female slaves by white male masters, the slave population has increased to become the largest single ethnic group in the country [Mauritania]...[34]

I met Abdi in his master's shop near Cheikh Anta Diop University in Dakar on August 3, 1994....Established in 1958, the university is one of the oldest and most prestigious education centers in West Africa. Obviously, Abdi did not end up here to learn to join the few elites of the region. He was brought here from Mauritania by his master, who was seeking profit. The master can work him to death with impunity and then send for another slave.

Shockingly, no one seems to notice that a black slave is still being kept in bondage, right in the heart of Dakar, by his Moorish enslaver. The modern chaos brings certain freedoms to the rapidly growing informal business underworld. Like in many other parts of the continent, the colonially created state of Mauritania is withering away. The role of the state has been reduced by the IMF and World Bank conditions that ensure the dictator's protection from being lynched by the hungry and angry urban masses. So, the Moorish master is not worried at all that this capital crime might be discovered, or that people passing by his shop might hang him in the tree growing just outside...[35]

Abdi is not responsible, nor is he a human being with feelings or the right to make a family. He is a machine that works like hell without pay or rest. Like the machine, Abdi needs only to be fed to oil his black muscles from cracking. His master can take him anywhere and make him carry out any task. He can be legally sold, given away, used to pay a bride price, or castrated to avoid mating with the master's harem.

The master's right comes before that of God, and he has the right to sleep with any of Abdi's female relatives, as they are by law his concubines. Abdi is not even allowed to go to the mosque if his master needs him...

The vast majority of the slaves are so brain-washed, that they would consider it a sin to escape from their masters. Their ancestors were kidnapped into slavery long ago, and their offspring have been brought up to believe that Allah created two groups of people: slaves and masters, each playing specific and eternal roles in society.

Abdi, another slave and their master had come to Dakar some years ago. Perhaps the master intended to use his slaves as starting capital for his business. Small businesses thrive and bring quick profit, especially for a foreigner with free slave laborers who can melt in as Senegalese in Dakar. There are no state-controlled opening hours, so the two slaves work almost 24 hours day, and eat and sleep inside the shop in shift[s].

I coincidentally stopped by the shop to buy a drink. Abdi was busy selling basic items to customers from the university. There was another man helping Abdi. I recognized them as Mauritan-

Abdi (top) *and co-slave working in their master's shop*

ian slaves because they were black and spoke the Arabic dialect of the white Moor community of Mauritania. This made me curious to want to talk with the two men about their business in Dakar. Without telling them that I was actually Mauritanian like themselves, we conversed across the counter of the shop. But they were hesitant to my inquiries concerning their life in Dakar and the situation in Mauritania. After a while though, they said that they were running the shop "together" with their master. I wondered where the master was. Abdi smiled and pointed behind the counter.

There he was, a little shabby looking white Moor, sleeping (see photographs above) while his two black slaves toiled for him. Before he woke up, I was able to steal a couple of shots of him and his two slaves...[36]

In Search of Answers

My research thus far had yielded a picture of a slavery that was both primitive and sophisticated, overt and subtle. It had also raised an abundance of questions, some of which I had no answers for, and others whose answers forced painful yet critical revelations.

My questions were moving me from a study of slavery in Mauritania and Sudan to a larger analysis of Islamic law and the Qur'an's perspective on race. I sought to understand more clearly the complexities of the sub-Saharan slave trade and how the Arabs organized and ran it. I also sought to determine the origins of Arab racism. Did the Qur'an support such racist perspectives? I wondered. If not, then how did Mauritania's Beydanes come to hate black Africans so, and why had they been so successful in enslaving them, and for so long?

I began to realize that I was tackling an extremely complex and explosive issue. My investigations of the continued existence of slavery in Africa promised to lay bare an ideological, political, and religious minefield.

I knew that a number of people might conclude that my article would represent an unfounded attack on Islam. The fact that both the Arab slaveholders and the African slaves whose wretched conditions I planned to expose were Muslim would not matter. Some members of the Nation of Islam, black orthodox Muslims, and the American and international Arab and African communities were going to take this personally! Of course, for these groups, it was alright to discuss Christianity's role in the enslavement of black people, but it was not alright to discuss what the Arabs, under the pretext of Islam, have done and were clearly continuing to do

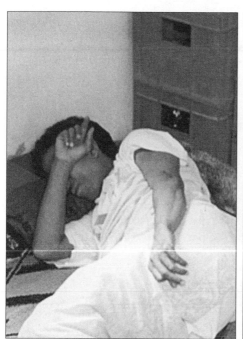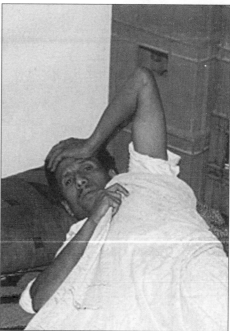

*The master is taking a nap behind the counter of his shop in which he exploits
the blacks 24 hours, as there are no opening/closing regulations in Senegal*

in northwestern Africa.

I was also beginning to realize that the relationship between Arabs and
Africans is not an easy subject for the African-American community. For the
most part, it is a taboo subject. This was clearly going to be an emotional
and volatile ride—the start of a much-needed dialogue—and not a pleasant
one! I had to be sure of what I was doing.

▩   ▩   ▩

I knew I was setting a course that would lead me into a confrontation
with people who would not want to deal with what was certain to become
an ugly subject. I wanted to stop my writing. This project was getting larger and larger and becoming more demanding.

Yet, something was happening to me. I was beginning to understand
why black people needed to know and thoroughly understand as much
as possible about the history and culture of Africa. With that in mind, I
prepared myself to make an investment of considerable intellectual capital
in that area of study. Only then, I realized, could I make an honest and sincere effort to understand and explain African slavery in its modern form.

CHAPTER THREE

The Arabian Peninsula, that vast area stretching from the border
of Russia to the Persian Gulf and the Red Sea and westward to
the Mediterranean, was always a market for slaves. Over the centuries many millions of white and black people of scores of races have disappeared into its mysterious towns and desert wastes....It is hardly
necessary to explore the history of slavery in Saudi Arabia as we did in the
Sudan; the larger, deeper history is well known and recorded. Saudi Arabia and her neighbors provide a study of modern slavery under entirely
new conditions.[1]
    —JOHN LAFFIN, *The Arabs as Master Slavers*

Before I could begin writing this controversial piece for the *City Sun*, I
wanted some questions answered. First, I wanted to know how, with a clear
conscience, a person calling himself a Muslim could not only enslave his
black spiritual brother but also reduce that slave to the level of an animal—
in an Islamic setting? Second, I wondered, is this behavior supported by the
Qur'an? Third, what effect has Arab racism had on the mind of black
Africans, both slave and free, down through the centuries, and what are its
implications today?

My fourth, fifth, and sixth questions were even more probing and
complicated: How did the paradigm which states that blacks are "natural slaves" develop in the Arab world? What were the peculiar features of the Arab slave trade? And how did it differ from the European
slave trade?

There were still other questions on my mind. Why was it that white Christians and Jews are fair game in some black folks's historical discussion of the enslavement of black people, while many blacks shy away from discussing the Arab's role in enslaving their African neighbors? Why could we talk so openly and passionately about the atrocities of one master and not another?

Even further, I wondered why so few critical questions had been raised about Arab slave-holding over the years. Was it because many feared that criticizing those who claim to worship Islam and yet who continue to enslave, torture, rape, and murder African people would make them an enemy of Islam?

Why were my instincts telling me that this article was going to cause me trouble?

❖   ❖   ❖

Not only were the answers to my background questions important to me as a researcher and a journalist developing a news series on a sensitive issue, they were important to me as a black man who would be examining a part of history that many blacks, both Christian and Muslim, do not feel comfortable discussing. I had never before explored such a dark corner of black history, and it struck me as strange that so few blacks had done so or even dared to explore the truth behind Africa's shameful secret.

ISLAM AND RACE

In his book, *Race and Color in Islam*, Bernard Lewis maintains the following:

> There is a distinction which it is important to make in any discussion of Islam. The word Islam is used with at least three different meanings, and much misunderstanding can arise from the failure to distinguish between them. In the first place, Islam means the religion taught by the prophet Muhammad and embodied in the Muslim revelation known as the Qur'an. In the second place, Islam is the subsequent development of this religion through tradition and through the work of the great Muslim jurists and theologians. In this sense it includes the mighty structure of the Shari'a, the holy law of Islam, and the great corpus of Islamic dogmatic theology. In the **third** meaning, Islam is the counterpart not of Christianity but rather of Christendom. In this third sense, Islam means not what Muslims believed or were expected to believe but what they actually did—in other words, Islamic civilization as known to us in history.[2]

It was Lewis's second and third perspectives that shed the greatest light for me on the origins of racism in the Arab world and the Arab justification for enslaving blacks in Mauritania and the Sudan. Coupled with my study of Islam and my conversations with devout Muslims prior to writing my article, Lewis's research helped one point to emerge as crystal clear: just as there are those in Christendom who have shouted the Gospel while spreading and fortifying slavery throughout Africa, Europe, and the Americas, there are those Muslims who have cloaked themselves in piety while shackling the bodies and lives of African people.

Yet, neither the words of Christ nor the Islamic prophets set any precedent or provide any rationale for the existence of racist thought. While the Qur'an and certain pieces of ancient Arabian poetry reveal that the Arabs were aware that they were distinct from the Persians, Greeks, and other national and ethnic groups with whom they came into contact, there is no clear indication that they perceived themselves or others in racial terms.[3] The Qur'an expresses no racial or color prejudice within its pages. Only two of its passages even address the issue of human diversity. The first is Surah 30, Verse 22, which reads:

Among God's signs are the creation of the heavens and of the earth and the diversity of your languages and of your colors. In this indeed are signs for those who know.

In its reference to the many colors of mankind, this verse is expressing Allah's power to create a world of great diversity. The second passage is found in Surah 49, Verse 13:

O people! We have created you from a male and a female and we have made you into confederacies and tribes so that you may come to know one another. The noblest among you in the eyes of God is the most pious, for God is omniscient and well informed.

This passage leads worshippers to appreciate the contention that, in the eyes of Allah, it is not the group that one is born into or one's color that makes the difference, but rather the depth of one's devotion to Allah's words and commandments.[4]

How, when, and where, then, did Arabs, particularly Mauritania's Beydanes, come to develop the perspective that black Africans were inferior and thus suitable for enslavement?

❋   ❋   ❋

Historians such as Bernard Lewis report that under the patriarchal *caliphs*, who were the successors of Muhammad, a radical and racist perspective began to emerge.[5] As a prophet, an instrument of revelation, and messenger of Allah, Muhammad could have no true successor. Thus, in Islamic thought, succession to Muhammad meant succession to the sovereignty of the State. The first caliph, Abu-Bakr, began his rule in 632 A.D. and was succeeded by various caliphs until the appearance of the Umayyad dynasty, which ruled from 661 A.D. until approximately 750 A.D.[6] According to Lewis:

> Several Arabic poets of the pre-Islamic and early Islamic periods are described as "black," and are known collectively, to the literary tradition, as **aghribat al-Arab**: "the crows of the Arabs." Some of them—mostly pre-Islamic—were Arabs of swarthy complexion; others were of mixed Arab and African parentage. For the latter, and still more for the pure Africans, blackness was an affliction. In many verses and narratives, they are quoted as suffering from insult and discrimination, as showing resentment at this, and yet to some extent as accepting the inferior status resulting from their African ancestry.[7]

One such voice of acquiescence belonged to the black African poet Suhaym (d. 660). Born a slave, Suhaym's name means "little blackie." In one poem, he laments: "If my color were pink, women would love me, But the Lord has marred me with blackness." In another, he writes: "Though I am a slave my soul is nobly free, though I am black of color my character is white."[8] Lewis continues:

> Probably the last of the early black poets in Arabic was Abu Dulama (d. ca. 776), a slave who became the court poet—and jester—of the first Abbasid caliphs. In his verses, the acceptance of inferiority is unmistakable. To amuse his master, Abu Dulama makes fun of his appearance, of his aged mother, and of his family—"We are alike in color; our faces are black and ugly, our names shameful."[9]

These passages reveal that through the centuries, black Africans absorbed the perspectives of their Arab conquerors. Such perspectives would wreak havoc on their self-perception as time wore on, as reflected in a *Newsweek* interview with Mauritanian slaves. In that interview, a slave named Dada Ould Mbarek made the following comments:

> He was asked: **Weren't Mauritania's slaves emancipated?** "I never heard of it," he said. "And what's more, I don't believe it. Slaves free? Never here." **Isn't he the same as his master?** "No, I'm different. A master is a master and a slave is a slave. Masters are white, slaves are black." **Is this just?** "Naturally, we blacks should be the slaves of the whites."[10]

DEVELOPMENT OF THE ARAB RACIST PERSPECTIVE

As Bernard Lewis notes: "According to the doctrines of Islam—

repeatedly reaffirmed by the pious exponents of the Faith—the non-Arab converts were the equals of the Arabs and could even outrank them by superior piety."[11] My own research, however, suggested that this may have been true in theory, but it certainly was not true in practice. Instead, Arab Muslims have behaved similar to other conquering peoples. That is, they have been—and apparently remain to this day—highly resistant to giving equality to those whom they have vanquished. They have long looked upon subjugated non-Arab Muslims as inferior and have historically subjected them to a wide range of fiscal, social, political, and military pressures.

The struggles of two groups to gain equality in Arab society are important to grasp for an understanding of slavery in northwestern Africa: that of non-Arab converts to Islam and that of persons of mixed Arab-African descent. For example, while the lighter-skinned Persians and Syrians faced barriers to equality after being conquered by the Arabs, they eventually gained full entry into Arab society due to the increase in their numbers over time. This has not been the case for Mauritania's Negro-Africans. Their high visibility and the stigma attached to black skin in the Arab world have served to keep them at the bottom of Mauritanian society. As Lewis writes:

> *The son of an Arab father and a Persian or Syrian mother would not look very different from the son of two Arab parents. The difference was in effect social and depended on social knowledge. The son of an African mother, however, was usually recognizable at sight and therefore more exposed to abuse and discrimination. "Son of a black woman" was a not-infrequent insult addressed to such persons, and "son of a white woman" was accordingly used in praise or boasting.*[12]

Lewis goes on to relate the story of the half-mythical poet 'Antara, the son of an Arab father of the tribe of 'Abs and a black mother. According to legend, 'Antara was extremely proud of his connection to an Arab father, who later emancipated him. He was also aware of the stigma associated with his black mother, and bore an intense hatred for full-blooded black African slaves. Lewis offers a verse ascribed to 'Antara, which states: "I am a man, of whom one half ranks with the best of 'Abs. The other half I defend with my sword."[13] In this regard, 'Antara is the forerunner of the Haratine "black Arabs" of Mauritania and the "brown Arabs" of Sudan, both of whom have internalized racist Arab perceptions of black Africans. Indeed, after centuries of slavery, these Africans' lowly perceptions of themselves mirror those of their Arab masters.

Virulent strains of racism and prejudice were alive and active in the pre-Islamic period as well. Not only Africans, but dark-skinned Arabs and Arabs of mixed African parentage suffered and were adversely affected by it. For example, when referring to blacks, Al Masudi (d. 956), a Muslim writer of the tenth century, relied on the authority of the Greek physician and medical writer Galen (d. circa 199 A.D.). Masudi states that Galen attributes ten specific attributes to the black man:

> *...frizzy hair, thin eyebrows, broad nostrils, thick lips, pointed teeth, smelly skin, black eyes, furrowed hands and feet, a long penis and great merriment....Merriment dominates the black man because of his defective brain, whence also the weakness of his intelligence.*[14]

Such negative perceptions of blacks would persist even though some Muslim writers attempted to offer balanced accounts of blacks based on personal knowledge acquired by contact with African kingdoms. A Persian treatise on world geography, written in 982 A.D., represents the common perception of most Muslim writers about the blacks of Sudan. According to its author:

> *Most of them go about naked. Egyptian merchants carry there salt, glass and lead, and sell them for the same weight in gold....In the southern parts there is no more populous country than this. The merchants steal their children and bring them with them. Then they castrate them, import them into Egypt, and sell them. Among themselves there are people who steal each other's children and sell them to the merchants when the latter arrive.*[15]

Consequently, Africa was perceived by the Arabs as a land inhabited by an inferior people, whom they called the *Zanj*, a term that summed up the worst of Arab perceptions of Africans. A word of disputed origin, Zanj was typically used to describe the Bantu-speaking peoples in East Africa south of Ethiopia. However, it was sometimes used more loosely to refer to black Africans in general, along with the general heading of "the Sudan," or "land of the blacks" or "blacks." The Zanj were the least respected, the Ethiopians the most respected, while the Nuba and Bujja (or Beja) occupied an intermediate position of respect.

The thirteenth century Persian writer Nasir al-Din Tusi remarked that the Zanj differed from animals only in that "their two hands are lifted above the ground." As he further claimed: "Many have observed that the ape is more teachable and more intelligent than the Zanj."[16] In his guidebook on slavery, Muslim scholar Ibn Butlan offered practical advice to prospective slaveowners about the Zanj. "The blacker the women," he wrote,

> *...the uglier their faces and more pointed their teeth...dancing and rhythm are instinctive and ingrained in them. Since their utterance is uncouth, they are compensated with song and dance....They can endure hard work...but there is no pleasure to*

be got from them, because of the smell of their armpits and the coarseness of their bodies.[17]

From the Arab perspective, then, the land of the Zanj was seen as a legitimate source of slaves. Enslavement of such debased beings, given that it resulted in conversion to Islam, was thus a beneficial and laudable practice.

This attitude is exemplified in the story of a black pagan king who was tricked and kidnapped by Muslim guests whom he had befriended. The king was later sold into slavery in Arabia. Meeting the guests again years later, the slave who was once a king showed contempt but no resentment for his captors because they had been the means of bringing him to Islam.[18] This perspective is still held by many Arabs, Haratines, and mixed-blood Africans of northwestern Africa today.

A case in point is Sheik Hassan El Turabi, an African with Arab blood, and the real power and architect of Islamic fundamentalism or revivalism in northern Sudan. In an interview with Rory Nugent of Spin magazine, El Turabi explained why he viewed black Africa as "virgin land" and an easy target for religious conquest:

Africa is fertile, ripe for the Islamic seed....In Africa, Islam's roots will go deep and become sturdy quickly. There is much to tap and little to compete with....What is there in Africa but tribalism?....We want to plant civilization in southern Sudan and beyond. They need one.[19]

El Turabi's comments reflect a racist perspective that historically has denied black Africa's rich cultural heritage. Today, this perspective justifies the processes of Arabization and Islamization that have been forced upon tens of millions of Africans in Mauritania and the Sudan.[20]

THE ARABS AND SLAVERY

Claud Anderson's work, *Black Labor, White Wealth*, makes an important point about the relative participation of various national and ethnic groups in the enslavement of African people. From an historical perspective, he indicates, virtually the entire world—the English, Portuguese, Dutch, Spanish, Africans, even the American Indians—participated in the African slave trade as either slave owners or slave traders.[21] Strangely enough, even the Chinese were participants, as early as the eighth century[22]; and Ethiopian slaves, known as *habshis* or *siddis*, were much sought after by East Indians as soldiers and sailors during the fifteenth century.[23]

❖ ❖ ❖

These historical realities are part of the African past and cannot be changed. However, the saga of the Arab slave trader and slave holder and his relationship with the black African transcends time. While every other group throughout the world has stopped enslaving black people, some Arab groups, specifically those in Mauritania and the Sudan, continue in this loathsome practice to this day. Significantly, these groups have never been chastised by others in the Arab world for their trading in black flesh.

According to David Brion Davis, in his book, *Slavery and Human Progress:*

> Moslems from the Middle East have enslaved and sold into North African slave markets no less than one million black Africans every 100 years, for the past 1,000 years....This practice represents no less than 10 million blacks enslaved and exploited by one group alone. Ironically, most Black African countries converted to the Islamic faith during the fourteenth century. Therefore, the Arabs' continuous enslavement of Blacks must be driven by factors other than blacks' religious faith.[24]

What are these factors? Clearly, in the case of present-day Mauritania, the continued enslavement of blacks who have been Muslims for generations is not for the advancement of Islam. We know this because Islamic law states that slaves taken in a holy war are to be released after conversion.

Claud Anderson may have struck at the core of the matter with his conclusion that "color was [and is] the decisive factor in slavery" in northwestern Africa and elsewhere.[25] In Anderson's view, the Arabs have used color as a means to an end in the following fashion:

> Arab expansionists adopted specific strategies. [Their] approach was to avoid confrontation and gain greater access to African wealth though intermarriage, concubinage, trade and religious proselytizing missions advocating one religious brotherhood. With the Black Moors and Islamic converts, the Arabs began their penetration of Africa. Often they exerted religious pressure and continually fostered holy wars that weakened the great West African empires....Arabs labeled Black Africans pagans, then pressured them to disavow their own West African culture and practice of ancestor worship and to accept instead Arabic culture based in the Islamic religion. This cultural and religious conversion undermined blacks' African heritage and broad sense of a black community. Moreover, the religious conversion to the Islamic faith gave Arabs nearly unrestricted access to West African societies and wealth.[26]

This successful Arab approach to controlling Africa continues to this day. It is against this nightmarish formula of historical oppression and destruction that Mauritania's black Africans, both slave and free, are struggling.

❊ ❊ ❊

From where I stood, African-Americans had a critical role to play in Africa's recovery. Yet, without complete knowledge of what really happened in the African past and of how that past affects Africa's standing in the world today, our contribution would be worthless. Though most African-Americans have knowledge of the African Diaspora that resulted from the trans-Atlantic slave trade, few black pundits or scholars have addressed or seen fit to teach us about an area of African history that is critical to our understanding of the slave experience: that of the lost Diaspora of northwestern Africa.

It was into that dark region of history and geography that I delved next.

THE LOST DIASPORA

To explain the relatively small numbers of black Africans presently found in northwestern Africa, some scholars have falsely argued that only a few blacks were brought across the deserts by Arab slave traders. These scholars would do well, however, to examine the high slave mortality rate reported by other observers and researchers of this trade. As Thomas Sowell states in his book, *Race and Culture*:

> *More African women than men were enslaved in the Islamic world, just the opposite of the situation among Africans taken in bondage to the slave societies of the Western Hemisphere, and these women were typically restricted from having sexual contact with men. The net result was that relatively few Black children were born in the Middle East, and very few survived to adulthood. Thus, despite the fact that even more vast millions of slaves were taken from Africa to the Islamic countries of the Middle East and North Africa over the centuries than to the Western Hemisphere, there is no such black population surviving in these Islamic nations today as the 60 million people of African ancestry living in the Western Hemisphere.*[27]

Part and parcel of this hidden legacy is a common tactic employed by the Arab slave traders. That practice was and is to condition and brainwash their African slaves from a young age such that they willfully participate in the enslavement of other Africans. For example, in his book, *Slavery in the Arab World*, Murray Gordon notes that it was not uncommon for these corrupted Africans, at the direction of their Arab masters, to launch fierce predawn *razzias* (raids) on unsuspecting villages in the African interior. In these raids, they would kill off many of the men and older women and march off the young women and boys to Arab-controlled assembly points.

From there, the newly subjugated Africans would be forced to begin the long trek across the Sahara Desert to the slave markets in North Africa. Those who were unable to walk were killed.[28]

As Arab scholar Abdullahi Mahadi points out about these raids and their consequences:

> Young girls and boys were preferred. Young girls to satisfy the sexual desires of indolent rulers and rich men in North Africa, the Near East and the Sudan. The young boys were desired, because of their ability to adapt to new environments and partly because they were more suitable for castration. The Sudanic and Arab ruling classes were determined to produce as many eunuchs as possible because the child could fetch as much as 250 or 300 dollars.[29]

The death rate among slaves en route to the slave markets was very high. An estimated twenty percent did not survive the trip, a fact grimly attested to by the thousands of skeletons that European travelers reportedly found scattered throughout the desert between central Sudan and North Africa in the 1850s. As one of these travelers noted, so strewn with the skeletons of human beings and camels was the route from Teggery in Fezzan (now southern Libya) to Kukawa (the capital city of Bornu, an old and strong African kingdom west of Lake Chad and notorious for its production of eunuchs), "an explorer unacquainted with the tract across the desert might almost without guide find his way by their aid."[30]

Another European visitor to northern Africa, Gustave Nachtigal, made the following observations about the toll of the desert trek on the enslaved Africans:

> ...the long journey, combined with inadequate food and scarce water, the contrast between the rich natural resources and humidity of the slaves' homes and the dry, wasting desert; the exertion imposed by mounted masters on slaves, mainly women and children, who trudged on foot, and the circumstances in which they suddenly found themselves, wasted away their youthful strength. Memories of the home they had left behind, fear of the unknown future, endless journeys, beatings, hunger, thirst and deadly fatigue drained them of all resistance. If they lacked the strength to get up and move on again, they were simply abandoned and their spirits slowly died. Under the destructive effect of the sun's rays, hunger and thirst, they quickly passed away.[31]

Jean Louis Burckhardt was another observer of the Arab slavers' treatment of their chattel. Funded by the African Society of London, Burckhardt was an extremely brave and resourceful explorer. He lived and traveled in the slave-hunting territories of Africa and in many parts of

Arabia from 1809 to 1817 and produced seven massive volumes about his experiences. To prepare for his journey, he spent two-and-a-half years in Syria, studying the Arabs there and learning to speak Arabic as if it were his native tongue. Dressed as an Arab or a Turk, Burckhardt often passed himself off as a poor Syrian sheikh with powerful friends. All the while he was aware that if his masquerade had been uncovered, he would have been killed for discovering and exposing the truth about the Arabs' treatment of their African slaves.

From the beginning of his travels in Egypt and the Sudan, Burckhardt claimed that the Arab-controlled African slave trade in northern Africa was far more serious than the trans-Atlantic slave trade, which was dominated by the Europeans. In his view, the Arab practice was bigger, more brutal, and, unlike slavery in the Americas, partly a religious perversion. Importantly, Burckhardt exploded the myth that Arab slave traders respected the chastity of the women they captured. He reported that it was only in public places and in the presence of European visitors that this appearance of decency was projected.

Burckhardt recorded the activities of a slave caravan as it made its way from the Sudanese interior to the port city of Suakin. At night, he stated, the caravan would camp in one large circle as protection against bandits. This configuration would create a makeshift arena where "scenes of the most shameless indecency" unfolded, and orgies of rape and debauchery would go on throughout the night while "the adult male negroes lay powerless shackled in irons."[33] Slavers would also sell the "use" of their female slaves to fellow dealers or to other merchants traveling with the caravan, Burckhardt claimed. As a result, few girl slaves older than ten reached their destination as virgins.

Burckhardt often likened the life of slaves to that of animals. He frequently wrote of seeing "gangs of slaves driven through the city to the market, where they lived in fetid filth and abject misery, crowded together as if in sheep-pens."[34] He was particularly sorry for the girls and young women who were herded through the streets in this manner. He noted with disdain that female African slaves thus herded, wearing nothing but a piece of tattered cloth around their waists, could barely endure the torments of the Arab street boys who poked or pulled at them while shouting obscenities.

Among the slave girls Burckhardt found many *mukhaeyt*: girls whose vaginas had been sewn up by the Arab slavers or market merchants. He noted that this operation may have taken place years before the sale so that the flesh had "agonisingly joined up."[35] The girls were left with a small orifice for urinating—their menstrual distress can only be imagined. However, he claimed, "Girls in this state are worth more than others; they are usually

given to the favourite mistress of the purchaser and are often suffered to remain in this state during the whole of their life."[36] With their virginity so
well established, female slaves subjected to this treatment brought a high
price from male Arab buyers, who would have their new possessions' vaginas opened up to the extent they found most satisfying and then proceed to
rob these women of their virginity.[37]

Indeed, one of the most common reasons for acquiring slaves in the
Arab world was to exploit them for sexual purposes. The Arab's great demand for African concubines was reflected in the preponderance of African
girls and young women who fell victim to the Arab slave traffickers. In an
early account, the fourteenth century traveler Ibn Battuta notes that upon
setting out from Takedda in the western Sudan to the northern Moroccan
city of Fez, he passed a caravan of six hundred slave women. Gordon claims
that caravans made up largely or exclusively of black African girls and
women was not an uncommon sight on the trade routes linking Bilad as-
Sudan to northwestern Africa.[38]

This practice must be contrasted with those employed in the slave states
of the American South, where it was not uncommon for slaveowners to
keep one or more slave girls as mistresses. However, the primary purpose
of slavery in the United States was to provide, at an economical price,
black labor to work the cotton, rice, and other fields that were the economic backbone of the South. Thus, in the U.S., male slaves, who became the
main toilers in the fields, generally commanded a higher price than did
women slaves of comparable age and health. By contrast, the export to
the Muslim world of large numbers of young female slaves was a distin-
guishing characteristic of the Arab-controlled domestic slave trade in Africa.
To be sure, it was a conscious and compelling motive for Arab involvement
in that trade.[39]

THE EUNUCH SLAVE TRADE

Another aspect of Arab slavery was hideously different from the trans-
Atlantic slave trade: the castration trade, or the trade in eunuchs. In this
practice, the Arabs created a market for castrated males, who were pur-
chased to watch over the enslaved women, who were kept carefully se-
questered in the confines of the home or the harem. With the increase in the
number of harems, the need for eunuchs grew. Eunuchs could be sold anywhere from twice to ten times the price of ordinary black boys.[40]

Gordon reports that large numbers of desexed boys were walked or
transported by boat or caravan from the African interior to Muslim countries in the north.[41] He claims, for example, that in the early nineteenth century, an estimated one to two hundred boys between the ages of eight and

ten were castrated every year in the Upper Egyptian village of Abotig (Abu Tig) on the caravan route from Sudan to Egypt. He also notes, however, that Islamic law prohibited Muslims from performing the operation. As a result, castrating young boys became a task that fell to nonbelievers, to be done in their own countries. Among the most skilled of these surgeons were Coptic priests who lived and worked at a main castration center located in Zawiyat al-Dayr, a predominantly Coptic village near Asyut (Siout) in Upper Egypt. Under the primitive conditions in which castration took place and owing to the unskilled nature of the practitioners, only a small percentage of boys survived the operation, which usually involved complete amputation of the scrotum and penis, or, as the expression went, cutting the sex organs "level with the abdomen."[42] A survival rate of one in ten, a rate that German explorer Henryk Barth observed during his travels in Africa, probably comes closest to the actual figures.

Using this estimate, approximately one hundred African boys died as a result of castration for every ten who survived to live as eunuchs. Thus, the "creation" of seven thousand eunuchs would require the death of approximately sixty-three thousand little boys. By contrast, far more consideration was paid to Arab or European boys who were castrated. The latter often retained the ability to perform coitus, and a few even took wives and concubines.[43]

Abdullahi Mahadi comments on the explorer Gustave Nachtigal's observations on the Arab practice of castrating African male slaves:

> According to Nachtigal, one of the most powerful members of Borno's ruling class in the nineteenth century, Laminu, appears to have been sufficiently devoid of conscience to collect from time to time hundreds of boys and to subject them to castration, condemned though this is by Islam. The barbers who performed the operation are accustomed with a quick grip to grasp the whole of their external genitals in the left hand, and with the right to amputate them with a sharp knife. Boiling butter that is kept in readiness and poured on the flesh would staunch the bleeding of the unfortunate boys.[44]

Mahadi concludes by noting that many of these youth succumbed as a result of the horrible operation, and those who survived would be allowed only a few days rest before beginning their forced march through the Sahara.

In another historical report, the Arab Caliph al-Amin (809-813 A.D.) was alleged to have collected eunuchs in huge numbers and to have divided them into separate corps of white and black eunuchs called *jarradiyya* (locusts) and *ghurabiyya* (ravens), respectively. An Arabic description of the court of the caliph of Baghdad at the beginning of the tenth century speaks of seven thousand black and four thousand white eunuchs, the latter of whom the author notes soon became rare and costly in Africa.[45] In Egypt, where eunuchs were kept by the ruling family of Muhammed Ali and by rich Turks, castrated males were said to have brought a great price in the slave markets of Cairo and Alexandria.

To most Arab Muslims of those earlier centuries, transforming a black male child into a eunuch raised no more of a problem than enslaving a young African girl for life in a harem. The Arab rationale was that the African boy's station in life as a eunuch was far superior to anything he might have known as a free non-Muslim. The Muslim view was that the pain suffered by the child in losing his virility was more than offset by the benefits to be gained by being reduced to this servile state.[46] Chief among these benefits, they rationalized, were conversion to Islam and the loss of their African culture, traditional values, and identity.

◈　　◈　　◈

This bitterly painful legacy of the psychological, physical, and sexual exploitation of black men, women, boys, and girls at the hands of Arab masters is one of the many terrible truths about the African slave trade that I was confronted with as I prepared to write my article. It was a history of which I was totally unaware, one that no one—white or black, Christian, Arab, or Jew—had ever shared with me. I felt sickened, yet I knew I had to go on. I knew as well that what I was finding out was but one among many other bitter realities that people of Arab and African descent everywhere simply had to come to grips with.

As I finished this disturbing phase of my research, the lessons of African history were clear to me. I had a firm grasp and understanding of Mauritanian slave society, and I understood the historical underpinnings that determined the relationship between Africans and Arabs. I was also clear where Islam stood on the issue of race. I was ready to write my article.

I was sure that when the African-American community and its leaders learned of the existence of modern-day slavery in Mauritania and Sudan they would be, like me, justifiably outraged. Once they read about it in my article, I just knew they would rise up to take the actions necessary to end the enslavement of our brothers and sisters in Africa. Given our shared history of slavery, I was sure that news of the conditions that I would soon unveil would resonate in the hearts of every African-American.

I felt a sense of satisfaction. I felt that I had been given the privilege of informing black people about an issue they would want to—need to—know about. Sure, I thought, I would have to face some confrontations. Some of my Muslim brothers might become a little upset, maybe a little suspicious, when then heard about this. Still, when they saw the evidence I had compiled, they would have to put all their differences behind and take action to end modern-day forced servitude.

◈   ◈   ◈

I expected that everyone else would see things the way that I saw them. The truth of the matter, however, was that I was myself still blind to a certain extent.

I was still a contradiction. True, I had changed from a person with little or no interest in African history or culture into one firmly convinced of the importance of knowing all there is to know about my people's past and present realities. But when I finished my article, I fully expected to leave it behind and move on to another. There was nothing else for me to do, I thought then, about what was happening in Mauritania. I was only one person, and this slavery had been going on for a long time.

I would go on write about other issues other than slavery. I would go back to my comfortable and very private world and continue to entertain my aspirations of becoming a renowned journalist. I would let the black leaders and heavy hitters be the ones to go to bat and fight for the cause I had brought to light. I wouldn't have to do anything about it myself.

Well, as they say, "life is what happens while you are making other plans." What I thought was the end of my involvement with the Arab slavery issue was only the beginning of a chain of events that would change my life forever.

The research I was conducting in preparation for my article had begun to have a profound effect on me. It began to fill my waking hours and my dreams. The images of those ancestors—the men, women, and children who had suffered through times that were so terrible—along with the images of my contemporaries in northwestern Africa who were still enduring the hardships and drudgeries of slavery—would jar me awake in the middle of the night. They would compel me to rise from my bed and begin reading and writing. They were with me as I examined book after book on the topic. Their spirits transported me across continents to the arid wilderness of Mauritania and Sudan. I could feel the heat and the sorrow emanating from the caravans. Those deserts were the true killing fields.

◈   ◈   ◈

I prayed that the spirits of the African ancestors would come forth and fill the hearts and minds of those who would read my article, just as those spirits were coming to me with such urgency. Help my readers, I prayed to them, to better understand the past and present of African people, not only intellectually but spiritually. Let the souls of the dead who entered my bedroom at night speak through me to explain to my brothers and sisters the horrors our ancestors experienced in the sands of the Sahara.

CHAPTER FOUR

〰〰〰〰〰〰〰〰〰〰〰〰〰〰〰〰

*Y*ou run on ahead?—Do you do so as a herdsman? or as an exception? A third possibility would be as a deserter. First question of conscience.

Are you genuine? or only an actor? A representative? or that which itself is represented?—Finally you are no more than an imitation of an actor...Second question of conscience.

Are you one who looks on? or who sets to work?—or who looks away, turns aside...Third question of conscience.[1]
—FRIEDRICH NIETZSCHE

During the weeks that I was working on my article, I realized more and more that what I was writing was going to create a storm of controversy. The part of me that was a coward started kicking in, telling me that I had no business putting myself in the position of point man on this issue. I was beginning to feel extremely depressed and isolated from my colleagues in the media, especially the black media. Worse, I was tempted to water down the tone and substance of my article, to not word my indictments of the Mauritanian and Sudanese governments so strongly. I had a sense that I was sailing out into dangerous and forbidding waters. I was sounding an alarm that maybe no one in my community or the world wanted to hear.

On a day that I was particularly concerned about the potential back-lash, I called Andrew Cooper at the *City Sun*.

I asked Cooper if he was sure that he wanted to continue with this series. The information I was uncovering would shatter many preconceptions in the African-American community and probably make a number of people uncomfortable, I warned him. I told him that much of what I was discovering was very critical of America's black political and spiritual leadership, who, for the most part, had chosen to remain strangely silent on the issue. My research was also pointing out that black newspapers, magazines, and radio and television programs had expressed little or no interest in the contemporary slavery going on in Africa.

Cooper listened quietly until I finished talking. Then, after a few minutes, he simply laughed and replied that he didn't give a *damn* about people getting upset. He would *not* be intimidated! He wanted this story researched, and if it was true, he wanted it to break in the *City Sun*. He assured me that he would back me and take whatever pressures came as a result. "Sam, just keep on with your writing and research," he said.

◈   ◈   ◈

Still, I wondered if I was using good sense. I was a neophyte writer. Was I was being silly and idealistic? Why hadn't more experienced writers ever covered this story? Was it because they knew better than to explore a subject nobody wanted to talk about? Maybe they were smarter than I was. Maybe they had more sense than to set off an explosion that would make them a target of controversy.

I finally gained control of my fears by accepting that it was okay to be nervous and afraid as long as I remained committed to finding and telling the truth. If my article did that, I decided, I would submit it. If it did not, I would throw the whole works in the trash can.

Then at last the Friday evening came when I knew that I was finished. All that night I checked and rechecked my sources until I was sure that everything I had written was correct. By the first signs of dawn I felt at peace with myself. I had written a solidly documented article.

When I finally pushed back from my desk, I had before me a comprehensive, thoroughly researched piece of journalism that would be presented as a four-part series in the *City Sun*. I carefully removed the manuscript pages from my printer bin and placed them into a folder. Exhausted but jubilant, I said to myself, "That's it, Sam, no more writing. It's done now."

◈   ◈   ◈

I delivered my article to Maitefa the following Monday and waited anxiously for her response. She called me on Thursday to inform me that she was very happy with the piece. She then said something that I did not believe at the time: that my article would lead to radio and television appearances. I didn't believe that would happen. I had never been on radio or television before. I thanked Maitefa but told her that her prediction seemed a bit farfetched—I was more concerned about when the series would run. She said to look for it on the newsstands by the following Wednesday.

I hung up the phone with mixed feelings of excitement and trepidation. I was going to be up to my eyeballs in crocodiles when this material hit the stands. I asked myself, "When I come under attack and my work is scrutinized, will I be able to take the heat? Will my article stand up under pressure? Mostly, will they give voice to the thousands of Africans who were still suffering under the horrible, dehumanizing conditions I described?" I breathed a sigh of relief. As far as I was concerned, I had done my job. My moral obligation had been fulfilled.

❖   ❖   ❖

The Wednesday morning that the series was to appear, my eyes flew open bright and early. Immediately, I was out of bed, throwing on some clothes, and running out to the store to buy the paper. There it was! Wow! Andrew Cooper was certainly *not* a man to pull his punches! He had run the article as a front-page feature, and the large print of the headline seemed to jump off the page: "Arab Masters—Black Slaves: A *City Sun* Exclusive"[2]

I called my friends and family and told them to make sure they picked up a copy of the paper, but several of them told me that they were having a hard time finding it. I telephoned Maitefa and asked her what was happening. She told me that many of the newsstands, especially those located in Brooklyn, were operated by Muslims, and a number of stores that distributed the *City Sun* were operated by Arabs. When they saw the headline, they had either covered it up or taken the papers off their stands. Maitefa promised me that the problem would be cleared up soon because Gary Byrd, the host of the popular black radio talk show "Gary Byrd's Experience" on WLIB-AM, had commented favorably on the article and had encouraged his listeners to read it. She was certain that pressure from Byrd's listeners and other *City Sun* readers would force the vendors to sell the papers.

She was right. The next day, the issue was back on the stands, and just as quickly, folks started calling the paper's offices to inquire about it or register their comments. Things were starting to heat up.

❖   ❖   ❖

Maitefa phoned me on Monday and told me that a Mr. Akbar Muhammad, the international representative of the Nation of Islam, had called to complain about the article. He said that it constituted an attack on Islam and accused me and the *Sun* of being part of a "Jewish plot" masterminded by Charles Jacobs of the American Anti-Slavery Group. Muhammad swore that neither slavery nor trafficking in slaves existed in the contemporary Arab world. He was particularly incensed that my article implicated Muammar Al-Qaddafi's Libya in the practice of slavery. Muhammad's reaction was to be expected because, as I later read in Gilles Kepel's book, *Allah in the West: Islamic Movements in America and Europe*:

> *Links between the Nation of Islam and the Muslim world have always been important although, as we have seen, there have been ups and downs. When W. D. Muhammad [seventh son of Elijah Muhammad] was steering the movement "back on course" towards Muslim orthodoxy, Farrakhan had very severely criticized the Arab states which generously supported his rival, even calling them racist. Later, in 1985, having previously turned downs arms and access to Libyan training camps, Farrakhan received an "interest-free loan" of $5 million from Colonel Gaddafi to "overthrow our oppressor." The Nation of Islam leader made several trips to Muslim countries, and in 1985 was able to boast that he had made the pilgrimage to Mecca at the invitation of the general secretary of the Muslim World League, an organization aligned with Saudi Arabia, thus playing down his clashes over dogma with the leading Islamic authorities in the Middle East.*[3]

Curiously, Mr. Muhammad never attacked Tony Brown, the first black journalist to break the story. But with press releases and radio and television announcements, he began to unleash a firestorm of accusations at Andrew Cooper and myself. Cooper brought the following NOI press release to my attention. The release was entitled, "One More Big Lie: America Accuses Libya of Enslaving Black People," and dated March 24, 1995. It was written by Akbar Muhammad:

> *The western nations, namely, the American government, and special interest groups, specifically the United Nations, have caused the people of Libya untold suffering with inhumane sanctions and bombings. Now the American Anti-Slavery Group headed by Dr. Charles Jacobs, a Jewish consultant, has accused the Libyan government of selling Black people. In part two of a three-part article...written in the New York City Sun by Mr. Samuel Cotton, it states that in the country of Libya, Black people are being sold into slavery. Mr. Cotton went a step further than part one of his articles where he said that the President of Africa's largest country, the Sudan, has six to eight slaves in his home in Khartoum.*

An invitation has been extended to members of the Black press, including Mr. Cotton and his publisher, to visit the Sudan. To date, Mr. Cotton nor Mr. Andrew Cooper, publisher of the City Sun, has responded. Mr. Cotton's quotes and most of the information called "research" was obtained directly from the Anti-Slavery Group based in Washington, D.C., via Dr. Charles Jacobs. Dr. Jacobs has been using the pain of a Black Mauritanian to justify his attack on Islam, the religion. It is well known that the Blacks in Mauritania suffer under much racism and mistreatment by the rulers of this North African country. He is using this suffering to judge a religion and not the people of the religion. It is also an attempt to curtail and divide an already divided Black community on the issue of Islam and the influence of the Nation of Islam under Minister Louis Farrakhan.

The cartoon used in the article shows an Arab slave master beating a group of black men and women. Mr. Jacob has sent a press release to 95% of the African-American papers across the country. He is using the old FBI trick of planting stories. The Libyan people, who have a history of being wrongly implicated in activities that they have been vindicated from later, are still suffering from unjust sanctions imposed in April of 1992. These vindications have never been corrected in the eyes of the public nor by those who have imposed these sanctions.

Anyone who has read Muammar Al-Qaddafi's Green Book will attest to the fact of how he feels about Black people and their eventual ascension to a position of power in the world. He and the people of Libya have opened their doors to Black people from around the world and have struggled to show a true sense of brotherhood for Africans at home and in the diaspora.

As in all other cases, I am sure that this "Big Lie" being circulated by the American Anti-Slavery Group against Libya and the Sudan will be exposed as another manipulative device. I believe their propaganda is intended to continue to divide the Black and Arab people in America and on the African continent.

After issuing his press release, Muhammad contacted "Tony Brown's Journal" and requested a chance to tell his side of the story. He claimed that the *City Sun* and I were being used as puppets in a "Zionist plot" to attack Islam and impede its growth in the United States, to divide the black community over the issue of slavery, and to discourage business people from investing in Africa. He further accused us of helping to drive a wedge between the black community and the Arab community in both Africa and the United States.

Tony Brown agreed to let Mr. Muhammad appear on his show. He also invited me to appear. Soon afterwards, I received an invitation to debate Muhammad on Gary Byrd's radio show and to appear on other media programs.

Maitefa's prediction had come true.

FROM JOURNALIST TO ACTIVIST

In addition to the television and radio publicity generated by my series, I began receiving calls and letters from Mauritanian and Sudanese expatriates living in New York. Most of them thanked me and the *City Sun* for my articles. I became friends with many of these men and women, the first true friendships I had ever had with people from Africa. I did not foresee, however, that these new friendships would place a heavy burden of responsibility upon my shoulders.

When I wrote my articles, I had no intention of becoming an anti-slavery activist. My job, I believed, was simply to present the information to the African-American reading public. From there on, I saw it as the responsibility of prominent members of the black community like Minister Farrakhan, the Reverend Jesse Jackson, or the Congressional Black Caucus to address the issue. I figured that those individuals and groups who had waged such determined assaults against apartheid in South Africa would also rise to address the issue of slavery in Mauritania and Sudan once they had the facts. I had opened a door, but I wanted someone else, especially the Africans themselves, to walk through it and tell the world what was happening to them.

Nothing like that happened. It became increasingly clear that if I backed out of assuming an advocacy role for my enslaved brothers and sisters in northwestern Africa, they would quickly lose access to the media. I could not bring myself to do that. Although I was feeling a tremendous amount of pressure from various sectors in the black community for speaking out against the slaveholding Arab regimes, I knew that I was doing the right thing.

I remembered my fantasies as a little boy, those intense daydreams when I saw myself battling bravely to stop the slave traders from brutalizing my people. Well, the daydreams had come true. I was in a real fight against slavery, and, as in my dreams, the stakes were high.

❖   ❖   ❖

My newfound Mauritanian and Sudanese friends began to look to me as their spokesman. I began taking some of them to the radio and television shows I was invited to. Like Jacobs and Athie, I would present my research findings and then allow the Africans, many of whom could not express themselves well in English, to tell of their experiences. When they could not get their points across to the audience, I would speak for them. We were fighting together as a unit.

Before I knew it, I had, by a stroke of fate and the pull of conscience, stepped out from behind the writer's desk and become an activist in the struggle for African liberation. Still, I did not want to tangle with the Nation of Islam. Whenever I thought about backing out of my activism, it was for that reason. My African-American friends feared for my life. They warned me that many members of the Nation used to be criminals and worried that I was placing myself in danger for taking my stand.

I was torn because I respected the black Muslim organization's work in the black community and their courage in voicing the black experience. But I knew my friends were right. I knew too that African people were being enslaved and that the Nation of Islam was not being honest about what was really going on between blacks and Arabs in northwestern Africa. Despite a virtual flood of information, black muslims in America refused to acknowledge that their Muslim "brothers" in Africa were committing a grave violation of Islamic law. Worse still, they were not showing much concern for their fellow black Muslims in Mauritania and Sudan.

During the television interview on "Tony Brown's Journal," for example, Akbar Muhammad's criticisms of Charles Jacobs extended to his accusing Jacobs of trotting Mohamed Athie around "like a trained seal." At the time, I had only spoken to Athie on the telephone, but my later contacts and association with him would reveal a man who is far from being anyone's trained seal. The Mohamed Athie I came to know, like so many of the Mauritanian and Senegalese refugees I met as a result of my research, impressed me with his strong personality and clear sense of vision about what his country needed.

But even if black Muslims of the United States did not believe me and what I had to say about slavery in northwestern Africa, why didn't they believe my African comrades who were crying out so passionately about the issue? Why didn't they *join* me in protest?

At the time, I just couldn't understand. As a result, I was probably more mad than I was scared. I soon learned that when you understand this issue and hear the countless stories of the suffering these African people have borne, a suffering that has gone on for centuries, something happens to you inside. It suddenly does not matter that the people who are suffering are very far away. You somehow connect with them, and you are not afraid anymore.

❧   ❧   ❧

As an anti-slavery activist, I realized that I had strengths and weaknesses. My strengths lay in the fact that my research and writing about this issue were sound and comprehensive. My greatest weakness, however, was that I had never been to Africa. I had never seen firsthand the sufferings I was writing and talking about. Because of this, I was often stopped cold in my tracks when a radio or television commentator or another guest on one of the many talk shows I appeared on after my *City Sun* series hit the stands asked me the question: "Mr. Cotton, have you ever seen these things for yourself?"

The question used to frustrate the hell out of me. Usually, after it was asked, no one seemed to care about the mountains of documents and other evidence I had presented. My critics used this single point to discredit me and dismiss all of my sources as State Department and Zionist propaganda. Even after I stopped framing my arguments around State Department reports and other materials sent to me by Charles Jacobs, I soon realized that those who persisted in ignoring the remaining sea of data wanted nothing to do with the truth. For them, the weight of the evidence was irrelevant. This was not a struggle simply over whether I was right or wrong—it was a fight to stop the flow of information and discredit those who were speaking out on the issue.

My attackers claimed that I was being paid by shadowy sources for writing these articles. They claimed that I was part of a Zionist conspiracy to destroy Islam and divide people of African and Arab descent. It became clear to me that being black and working with a Jewish activist made me suspect in many corners of the black community, Muslim and non-Muslim. This created a dilemma for me because I was interested in working with anyone who was willing to strike a blow against slavery.

My life experience had not led me to believe that Jews were any smarter or better than I was. I had both competed against Jewish persons and worked with them on various projects in business and school, and had found that some are as capable as I am and some are not. Some have been good friends, and some have become enemies. Thus, I concluded that my critics' perceptions of the involvement of Jews like Charles Jacobs in the anti-slavery movement were not only racist and anti-Semitic, they also masked a form of self-hatred.

Such fears imply that Jewish people are categorically smarter than blacks, and that, in the presence of Jews, blacks lose their power for leadership and decision making. I didn't believe that. Nonetheless, with the Nation of Islam firing potshots left and right at Jacobs's credentials, credibility, and commitment to the struggle for African liberation, his effectiveness was being severely diminished. His messages about slavery and oppression in northwestern Africa were being clouded by the resentments and suspicions that some African-Americans still have about Jews.

Because I believed that black people needed to take the lead in this struggle, I worked with my African expatriate brothers and sisters to create a new anti-slavery and human rights organization in September 1995. We envisioned that this new organization—CASMAS, or the Coalition Against Slavery in Mauritania and Sudan—would become the flagship of the abolitionist movement. My only concern was: what role would Charles Jacobs and the American Anti-Slavery Group play in this struggle? We decided that Jacobs would continue to direct his organization and the two groups would keep sight of each other, but that CASMAS would set the agenda and the tone of the movement.

Jacobs was torn. On the one hand he wanted this to be a movement for everyone, and especially, I thought, an occasion for Jews and blacks to be once more together in a struggle for freedom. He had been in the civil rights movement. Attending Martin Luther King's "I Have a Dream" speech was, it seems, a high moment in his life.

On the other hand, Charles knew that at this moment in our struggle, his being a Jew gave the enemies of freedom an easy target and a way to deflect attention from the plight of the slaves. In the end, he agreed with us. He told us religious Jews (something he was moving to become) pray three times a day to a God who "matir asurim"—releases the bound, and that he felt commanded to do the most practical thing to achieve that.

In that sprit we pressed on—Africans, African-Americans and Jewish-Americans alike—to rid the African continent of slavery, once and for all.

THE POLITICAL GETS PERSONAL

The attacks on Jacobs and his involvement in the anti-slavery movement continued and broadened to include me and the *City Sun*. Representatives of the Nation of Islam intensified their adversarial stance and attempted to discredit my sources of information. Yusef Salaam, a Muslim reporter for the *Amsterdam News*, maintained that Andrew Cooper had been bribed with bank advertisements to run the series. He also stated the following:

I believe that a possible scheme behind Cotton's articles is to continue to loosen the ropes of his bit and allow him to venture into the quicksand in which Salman Rushdie is stuck, in hopes that the Muslim community in the U.S. will respond as the Muslims in Iran responded to Rushdie's writings....But Muslims will continue to ignore him in his efforts to polish falsehood into a shiny veneer resembling truth. The Muslims know that his sponsors will eventually cast him aside or assign him to another project.[4]

In a series of debates held on radio and television and at community forums, I repudiated these spokesmen and their theories about why the *City Sun* published my articles. I stood firm in my convictions, reminding them that in Mauritania and other parts of northwestern Africa, Muslim unity did not extend to their black brothers and sisters. I explained that the Arabs' culturally driven perception of blacks as slaves prevented them from granting black Africans the fair and proper treatment due them under Islamic law. An excellent example of this, and one that I frequently mentioned in these debates, is the wording of a contract for the sale of a black Muslim slave woman named Koumba Mint Sagheir and her daughter Kneiba in 1992.[5] That contract read as follows:

In the name of Allah most gracious and most merciful, salutation and peace upon him. Mohamed Vall Ould Nema son of Sidiba bought from Mohamed Lemine Ould Sidi Mohamed son of Taleb Ibrahim a slave with her daughter named Kneiba in the price of 50,000 Ouguiya received entirely by the seller from the buyer. Therefore, it becomes effective his property of the two slaves listed. The two parties did receive my witness and the buyer accepted before, the hidden defects of the slaves. The contract was made at the end of the month of Hija of the year 1412 [1992] by Abedrabou Montali Ould Mohamed Abderrahmane son of Berrou. God forgive me and my fathers and all the believers. — Here is the finger of the buyer's left hand.

After being informed of cruel realities such as these, the most common and immediate response of many of my African-American Muslim antagonists, particularly those who were members of the Nation of Islam, was to protect the image of their religion and their relationship with the Arab world. To my surprise, they displayed little concern or outrage about the destitution of their fellow black Muslims in Mauritania. Instead, they directed their anger at the black man who was bringing these conditions to their attention: me. Rather than protesting Koumba and Kneiba Sagheir's demise and criticizing the Arabs for their role in the enslavement of African people, they focused their suspicions on a purported Jewish "plot" to undermine Islam and Arab-African relations. They refused to accept the fact that Arabs, the central players in Islam, could do such terrible things to their fellow Muslims who are black, that they could be as racist and unscrupulous as white Christians.

Many of the black Muslims I debated mentioned the experiences that caused Malcolm X to change his perceptions about race in the Islamic con-

بســـم الله الرحمـــن الرحـــيم والصلاة والسلام على
النبي بعده

انشترى محمد وال بن النعم ابن دنيبة ابت مسا
عند محمد الامين بمشية محمد ابن ابی الطالب
من اهليه امة بينتها تسمى كنيب وابنتها
هذه زك صغيرة بثمن مبلغه خمسوك
وقفته حناز هاالبابها جميعا بامر رضا منـا
الشنتترى وتم ملكة الى كنيب المذكور نبـعالة
بهذا الشهدان ودخل المشترى على ايا فوطا
وكتب تاريخ اواخر ذالحجة سنة الاخ حمد
ربه مثال بن محمد عبذالرحان ابارخ عفى الله
لى ولـه الدى والله ۰۰۰ وابيا

سبابة البارح
البشرى

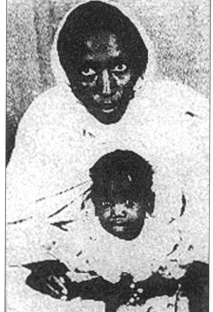

Xerox of original contract in Arabic

Koumba Mint Sagheir and her daughter Kneiba

text. They quoted Brother Malcolm:

> *America needs to understand Islam, because this is the one re-*
> *ligion that erases from its society the race problem. Throughout*
> *my travels in the Muslim world, I have met, talked to, and even*
> *eaten with people who in America would have been considered*
> *"white"—but the "white" attitude was removed from their minds*
> *by the religion of Islam....We were truly all the same (brothers)—*
> *because their belief in one God had removed the "white" from*
> *their minds, the "white" from their behavior, and the "white"*
> *from their attitude.*[6]

Yet, there I was, presenting example upon example that spoke to the contrary. "Are Malcolm's perceptions generalizable to the Arab world?" I asked, "The evidence says 'no!'"

I often cited a Mauritanian case reported in *Newsweek* in 1992. In that article, Fahl Ould Saed Ahmed, the Arab owner of two ten-year-old African slave boys, was asked if there was racism or slavery in his country. His reply: "There is no racism, there is no slavery." But that is not what the newsmagazine's researchers discovered. They reported the following: "In Mauritania, there is a Muslim ruling class made up of Berbers and Arabs, whose base is in the north of the country. They enslave thousands of blacks, who are cut off from their tribes in the south from their language and culture."[7]

I also frequently quoted from the work of Garba Diallo, an African scholar and Sunni Muslim from Mauritania, who makes a keen distinction between "Islam" and "Islamization." As Diallo explains:

> *The black Africans [in Mauritania] have the same cultural*
> *traditions as elsewhere in West Africa. What makes them slightly*
> *different is their thorough Islamization, which means that they*
> *sometimes confuse religion with Arab nationalism. They suffer*
> *from a serious identity crisis similar to that of the Arabicized Ber-*
> *bers of the country.*
>
> *The bulk of the blacks have lost important parts of their cul-*
> *ture as a result of confusion between nationalism and religion.*
> *This confusion makes them use Arab names when baptizing their*
> *children, instead of African names. It is ironic, that while com-*
> *plaining about black cultural chauvinism, blacks still glorify Arab*
> *symbols: names, language, etc. They do not seem to understand*
> *that these so-called Islamic names were authentic Arab names*
> *which were in use long before the revelation of Islam. Prophet*
> *Mohammed neither changed his name nor those of his followers*
> *following their conversion.*

Blacks in Mauritania have not fully realized that Islam is not the issue, it is just another means to an end. Successive regimes have capitalized on the black confusion to promote Arabization, join the Arab League, condone the practice of slavery, etc., ostensibly in the name of Islam.[8]

Yet, despite my wealth of evidence and reliance on carefully documented sources, Akbar Muhammad's most effective punch in our often lively debates was the simple question: Had I ever been to Africa and seen these things myself?

He was constantly challenging me to make the trip. He even offered to send me to Sudan as a guest of the Sudanese government. Of course, I could not accept his invitation. What could I possibly learn while traveling under the auspices of the very government that my sources alleged was guilty of gross human rights violations and of winking at the practice of slavery?

I realized that much of Akbar Muhammad's motivation was to protect the image of Islam and propel the continued growth of Islam in the African-American community, but I noted that whenever he suggested that I should journey to Africa, he always referred to Sudan or Libya. Never to Mauritania. He seemed intent on correcting or maintaining the image of these two countries and not the other. I wondered why. Maybe it was because he had no evidence to refute the practice of slavery in Mauritania.

I decided then and there to journey to Africa and to conduct primary research on my own—in Mauritania, the country Akbar Muhammad conspicuously ignored.

THE CHALLENGE

Two Mauritanian members of CASMAS, Mansour Kane and El Hadj Demba Ba, helped raise the money for my trip. Both were Muslims who had escaped persecution in their homeland and migrated to New York. Kane, a free or Negro-African and former army officer, had shared with me several horror stories of slavery and torture in Mauritania. He frequently spoke of Africans who suffered regular beatings, burnings, and even being buried alive at the hands of Haratines bent on carrying out the bidding of their Arab superiors.

Kane bore deep scars from his own encounters with the slavers and their lackeys. His ordeal began when the Beydane government began to purge blacks from the military in late 1990 and early 1991. He was arrested on November 18, 1990, and taken to the notorious Inal prison in the northern part of the country. There, he was tethered to the back of a truck and dragged mercilessly along a rocky road until, as his friend Ba recalled in a *Vibe* magazine interview, "his whole back was gone."[9] His amazing survival and recovery led Ba to proclaim proudly that Kane was among those special few who had actually cheated death and beaten it at its own game. "We say we only live once," Ba reflected, "but he [Kane] lives twice....He was dead and came back alive."[10] Kane survived, but 541 of his fellow soldiers weren't so lucky.

Prior to my trip, Kane and Ba developed valuable contacts for me with Mauritanian political groups, anti-slavery organizations, and with another important group, the African Liberation Forces of Mauritania (FLAM). They assured these organizations that I was safe to talk to and vouched for my character.

I would spend twenty-six days in Africa beginning December 22, 1995, and ending January 18, 1996. Because Kane and Ba didn't think it would be safe for me to travel with all my equipment through the south of Mauritania, they arranged for me to travel and live in Senegalese refugee camps just across the Senegal River. These camps were inhabited by Mauritanians who had been driven from their homes by the ethnic cleansing campaigns of the Arab government. I would also be spending ten days undercover, conducting research in Nouakchott, the desert capital of Mauritania.

I spent my days and nights before leaving meeting and talking with my new Mauritanian friends. I also did a lot of reading on the methodology of anthropological and ethnographic fieldwork. I did not want my investigation to amount to an hysterical attempt to force the truth. Instead, I wanted it to be based on direct observations and firsthand interviews with living members of an oppressed community. To do that, I would have to immerse myself in the realities of various groups of black Africans in Mauritania and Senegal, wear their traditional clothing, eat with them, live among them, and experience their conditions. Only in this way, I believed, could I achieve an honest conceptual understanding of what was really happening in northwestern Africa. Only then could I gain an understanding of the black experience that was not fashioned through an African-American lens.

Most importantly, only by going to Africa could I come to know for myself whether or not slavery and a unique form of racial apartheid was alive and well in my ancestral homeland.

CHAPTER FIVE

frica I have kept your memory Africa
you are inside me
Like the splinter in the wound
like a guardian fetish in the center of the village
make me the stone in your sling
make my mouth the lips of your wound
make my knees the broken pillars of your abasement...[1]
—JACQUES ROUMAIN

It is December twenty-third, and Flight 562 sets down in Dakar, the capital of Senegal. Senegal, the westernmost country in Africa, is bordered on the south by Guinea-Bissau and Guinea, on the east by Mali, and on the north across the Senegal River by Mauritania. The independent enclave of Gambia nearly divides the country. What is now known as Senegal and Mauritania was at one time one colonial territory before France divided it in two in December 1933. Senegal then became fully independent from France in 1960, the same year that Mauritania achieved its independence.

As I step through the door of the aircraft, the sun is shining brilliantly. A wave of heat washes over me as I put my foot on African soil for the very first time. "I am home, fathers and mothers! I am HERE! I have come as I said I would!" I feel like shouting. Instead, I say these words silently to my ancestors, my chest almost bursting, my heart flooding with emotion.

The ancient ones I am calling out to, I wonder, who were they? What were their names? What had they looked like? Making my way toward the terminal, I am completely absorbed by thoughts of that African man and woman who, after surviving that hellish voyage across the ocean, made love in a loveless world and brought forth the line that would bear the slave name Cotton.

After a few moments, I stop and turn full-circle around, looking closely for the first time at the land of my ancestors. Again to myself, I speak to those ancestors, the spirits that had brought me home, asking them to guide me and to make this trip a success.

I was in their hands entirely.

※　※　※

I needed an interpreter, pronto. I didn't speak French or any of the languages of Africa. I didn't know the people I was going to meet. How would they treat me? My mind was quickly filling with all kinds of questions: Would they be for real? Would they be nice people? How much English would they speak?

Once inside the terminal, I went to the line for new arrivals. A guard asked me for my passport, and after fumbling through my papers I found it. As I handed it over to him, my eyes feverishly searched the crowd for anyone who looked like they were looking for me. The guard asked me where I would be staying during my visit.

Damn, I thought to myself. My guide, a Mr. Mamadou Bocar Ba, was supposed to be here to pick me up. I didn't know where I was to be staying, he was to meet me at the airport and let me in on the details. Where was he?

There I was. I had come all that way, and I couldn't even get into the country! I turned to the guard and, in my hastily learned pidgin French, tried in vain to explain my situation to him. Suddenly, I felt someone tapping me on the shoulder.

"Tell him you are staying at Novotel," a deep male voice commanded me in English. "Tell him that."

I turned quickly to look at the man standing behind me and just as quickly turned back to the guard. "Novotel," I stammered. Then more firmly, "I am staying at the Novotel."

With that, the guard stamped my passport and indicated that I could pass through the gate. Talk about being relieved!

I turned back around to thank the African brother who had given me my directive. "Are you Mamadou Ba?" I asked.

"No," the smiling man replied, in almost impeccable English. "I'm just giving you some timely advice. Now, you'd better go and get your belongings."

I hurried to find my luggage.

❖   ❖   ❖

I spotted my suitcases on a moving conveyor belt amongst an assort-
ment of bags, boxes, and bundles, most carrying goods and appliances from
America. I looked around for a porter or someone who could help me with
my stuff. Seeing no one, I grabbed my bags and headed, struggling, for the
airport exit.

"Where are the brothers who said they would meet me here?" I wondered. "Did they come?"

I walked nervously toward the exit, sweating profusely from the intense
heat. Up ahead I could see a group of people, several of whom were waving
cardboard signs above their heads. My eyes scanned the crowd, and as I got
closer, I saw a most welcome sight. My name was written on one of those
placards, and beneath it were my contacts, two men who would soon become my close friends.

I had thought that Mamadou Ba would meet me as soon as I got off the
plane, but he informed me, in broken English with a heavy Francophone
African accent, that local folk were not permitted in that area. He haltingly
identified himself by his name and title, financial minister of FLAM, and introduced his compatriot, Abdoulaye Sy.

Sy was a tall, lanky man with a face that reflected such serenity and
kindness, I relaxed immediately in his presence. He spoke little English, so Ba
spoke for him, explaining to me that his friend was a former teacher.

Both men were obviously as happy to see me as I was relieved to see
them. They were friendly and warm, and I liked them right away. In the
days to come, during the many trips the three of us would make to the marketplace in Dakar, they would serve as my stalwart protectors and companions. To keep me from being robbed, one would walk in front of me with
the other behind. They would make me take my meals on time and remind
me to drink plenty of water to keep from becoming dehydrated.

They were like my brothers, these Muslims, and I was both grateful and
glad to be in their company.

MY FIRST DAYS IN AFRICA

At the airport, Ba and Sy hurriedly collected up my bags and hailed us
a taxi. Off we went into Dakar, sailing through a sea of Peugeots. Our destination, a section of town that was called Ouagou Niayes Two.

Jockeying for position and gaining speed, our driver rocketed us past
several makeshift markets. As we entered the city, however, our speed
quickly degenerated to a slow crawl. The cab moved sluggishly through
narrow, traffic-swollen streets. There seemed to be construction going on
everywhere, much of it looking as if the builders had run out of resources

Abdoulaye Sy (left) with Mamadou Ba

just before completion. Everywhere as well were scores of beautiful African women, each wrapped in splendiferous geles or headwraps and fabrics bedazzled by splashes of brilliant color.

Mamadou and Abdoulaye spoke calmly to each other in French as I sat glued to the window, staring out and thinking to myself: "These are the children of the people who were left when my forefathers were taken!"

As if from a distance I heard Mamadou calling my name, and I somehow pulled myself away from drinking in my first sights of Africa. Complaining about his English, he struggled to communicate with me. By two o'clock in the morning, however—after a long night of discussion about Mauritania, the struggles of his people, and the anti-slavery movement—I could understand him perfectly.

※   ※   ※

We arrived at the place where I was to stay in Ouagou Niayes Two, and I was introduced to two other men: Omar Ba and Bocar Ba. Like Mamadou and Abdoulaye, these two would also be of great help to me during my stay, especially the seventeen-year-old Omar, who had been designated to work as my research assistant. Omar was a bright young man with sparkling eyes and the command of six languages. Full of questions and quite mischievous, he was nonetheless a wonderful source of information.

Mamadou showed me around the house and led me finally to the small room where I was to sleep. It had a closet, a small desk, and a bed—the latter of which I discovered that night was the command post for an army of ticks. Still, I was comfortable in that little room, except in the evenings when huge waterbugs would leave the kitchen area and stop by for a visit by running underneath my door.

I was forewarned before I left New York that daily living in Africa would be far different from what I was used to, so I quickly adjusted to these and other realities. I tried to shut out the thought of waterbugs crawling over me at night and struggled to keep my mind on the business at hand. Besides, I told myself, I was meeting and talking with men who had been tortured and nearly killed for their beliefs. How could I go around, moaning and complaining about a few bugs, when they had faced and overcome such extreme challenges?

Mamadou suggested that I take my bath before dinner. He gave me a bucket and showed me where to draw water in the yard. He led me next to a tiny room furnished with only a small wooden bench. My bath consisted of taking off my clothes, standing on the bench, lathering my body with soap, and pouring the water from the bucket over me. As I was lathering myself, I happened to look up. To my surprise and shock, there was a squadron of mosquitos hovering just over my head! Needless to say, I immediately realized that showers in that part of the world were matters to be taken care of quickly.

After my bath, the five of us settled down to a communal meal and a seemingly endless conversation. It was well after midnight before I retired to my room. To protect myself from the mosquitos, I wore a sweatsuit to bed and covered my face with mosquito repellent. The sweatsuit idea wasn't so bad, really, because it gets very cool at night in Senegal, and the early morning hours are quite chilly.

I eventually fell asleep, only to be abruptly awakened by the music of male voices calling the faithful to worship. I looked at my watch. It was four o'clock in the morning and pitch black outside. I could hear Abdoulaye stirring in the next room. I called to him through my window, and asked him where he was going. He told me that he was going to the mosque to pray, and that he would return later to finish his rest.

I cannot describe how peaceful this close-knit Muslim community seemed to me and how safe I felt in Dakar. It was such a change. In New York, I recalled, Muslims were attacking my work and viewing me with suspicion. I had not felt comfortable or safe around them. Yet, here in

Omar Ba

Dakar, I was living with Muslims who had been worshipping Allah since their birth, and I felt that I was among friends who were thankful that I was there, fighting on behalf of Muslim people. In addition, everybody in Dakar greeted everyone else, and I mean everyone. It was not at all like the cold city of New York. Folks moved in and out of each others' homes with ease, and little children ran from yard to yard laughing and playing games. This was truly a community!

Mamadou, my primary contact, was a tall, slender, bearded man totally dedicated to the African struggle for liberation generally and to the care of the Mauritanian refugee community in Senegal specifically. But he was not a quixotic or emotional dreamer. No, he was a courageous and clearly pragmatic person, an action-oriented individual committed to destroying racism and its sister institution, slavery. And he had paid a heavy price for his commitments, journeying to the very edge of oblivion and back for a righteous cause.

A professor of physics and mathematics at a private school in Dakar, Mamadou's life was not the quiet life of a teacher. He described to me one evening the details of his arrest and torture at the hands of the Beydane government. It was in 1986, he told me, after he had been taken into custody for his human rights activities in Mauritania. In prison, he was subjected to the jaguar method of torture. First, the guards stripped him naked and placed an iron bar behind his knees. They then hoisted him upside down and suspended him by his knees with his hands and feet tied together. As he hung there, three guards took turns beating the soles of his feet bloody with a rod. When one became exhausted, another would rise to take his place until Mamadou lost consciousness. After the beating, they let him hang like that for hours. When they finally pulled him down, he could not walk and lay there naked in excruciating pain and humiliation for days.

He told me that others who have been forced to undergo the jaguar have had water thrown on them to revive them so that they could be subjected to more and more beatings. Some were left hanging until they succumbed from internal hemorrhaging.

The Mauritanian government sentenced him to approximately three years in prison. He spent fourteen of those months in the dreaded Oualata prison, where uncounted numbers of black Mauritanians have been tortured to death or so terribly brutalized that they never recovered. According to Mamadou, this type of treatment was commonplace for those blacks who resisted the process of Arabization that stripped and robbed them of their culture.

◈　◈　◈

My new friend's stories struck a familiar yet painful chord in my memory. I had heard of, read, and seen pictures of such torture and inhumanity in my earlier investigations. I decided to leave Dakar immediately for the refugee camps, and from there to slip into Mauritania to conduct more research.

LIFE IN THE REFUGEE CAMPS

On Monday, Mamadou and I began the long and arduous journey to the camps, located about four hundred kilometers from Dakar. We arrived at the first of these, N'Dioum, on Christmas day. We went next to Boki-Diawe', Wourossogui, and finally the Horkadiere refugee camp, arriving at the last by the twenty-seventh of December.

At the camps I saw firsthand how extremely difficult life had be-come for these dispossessed Africans. They were living in desolate areas with neither proper sanitation, adequate medical care, nor electricity. Yet, when I looked into their faces I did not see a defeated people. I saw a gentle but strong people, a people who radiated kindness and enthusiasm. You could very well enter that camp and not be able to connect to them the suffering and the horror they had experienced simply by observing their demeanor.

When I looked deeply into the faces of the men, women, and children in those camps I realized how we as a people had survived slavery and oppression. I saw in them living proof of the incredible power of African people to spring back from crushing adversity and manifest an incredible optimism. I learned from living with them how the human spirit could endure bone-crushing oppression and not become embittered—and indeed appear as if it had never, ever experienced the horrible things to which it had been subjected.

I also understood that this quality of resilience has been both a blessing and a curse to African people. On one hand, it is a factor that enabled us to endure slavery, but it is also one of the very reasons why we were enslaved in the first place—a deadly contradiction that I will explore in a later chapter.

According to my sources, black people remained enslaved in northwestern Africa, and that was what I was in Senegal and soon Mauritania to investigate. For the moment, however, I was spending my days and nights living among these strong and resilient refugees in their temporary shelters and camps. And something was happening to me. Living and talking with my Mauritanian brothers and sisters in Senegal was having a profound effect on my consciousness.

◈   ◈   ◈

Some nights I would lie awake and think to myself: Is this real? Where am I? I must be having a bad dream. But I was really there, in Africa. I wasn't at home in New York, reading about Africa in a book, magazine, or newspaper article. I was eating, sleeping, and living among Africans, in refugee camps. I was listening to them talk about their lives and sharing in their hardships. I was connecting with them, seeing and feeling what their lives were really like. Slavery and oppression were becoming real to me.

After a few days, however, I began to experience a strange and extremely intense mixture of emotions—sadness, anger, depression—feelings

Camp at N'Dioum

so powerful I was frequently overcome with fatigue. We were making the long trip from the Boki-Diawe' camp to the camp in Wourossogui. I had been thinking about how kind and friendly the men and women at Boki-Diawe' had been to me, and I started remembering the faces of all the children I had played with there.

I thought about the abject conditions they lived under, how they were forced to survive in those godforsaken places in the middle of nowhere with absolutely nothing to do, no work or recreation and no community infrastructure of any kind. I thought about the filth, the disorder, the chaos that was their existence. I felt it in my bones, in my flesh.

How could the way of life of thousands of folk—industrious farmers and their families whose farms and cattle had been stolen by the Mauritanian government simply because they were black and wanted to maintain their African culture—have been so violently uprooted and replaced by such madness?

Yet there I was, surrounded by some of the gentlest and most polite women and men I had ever met. These were people who had been tortured, raped, and, in some cases, castrated. They had next to nothing in the way of possessions, yet almost each and every one of them welcomed me into their makeshift huts like a long-lost relative.

All of a sudden, I felt dizzy, as if time were standing still and I was being swallowed up in it, all six-foot, one hundred-and-ninety pounds of me. Sucked into a black hole of insanity. Before I knew what was happening, I was crying like a baby.

❖   ❖   ❖

I remember one night, at the refugee camp in N'Dioum, as I was eating my evening meal with one of several communal groups. I was the guest of honor. There wasn't much food in the common bowl, and I was famished. Mamadou and I had traveled over torturous roads for twelve hours to get to our destination. As I hungrily sopped up the last bits of rice and meat from my section of the bowl, each of my hosts pushed their food to me, saying, "Yam, yam, Samba Kane!"—"Samba Kane" was the African name given to me by the Mauritanians. "Eat, eat!" they were telling me.

Members of other groups emptied their bowls in my bowl to make sure that their guest was full and satisfied. I was instantly humbled, and my emotions overwhelmed me again.

That evening is one of my fondest memories of Africa. But it was only one of countless times I bonded with the African people of Mauritania.

It happened again on the way to Wourossogui. It was early in the morning, and Mamadou was walking just ahead of me, leading the way to the point at which we would catch a bus traveling to the camp. Before me lay a broad expanse of virgin land, soaring trees, mountains, valleys. The scenery was new to me and should have been awe-inspiring. But I saw none of it. In my mind's eye all I could see was the faces of the men, women, and children I had left behind in Boki-Diawe'. I just couldn't help it, I started to cry. I tried to hide my tears, but Mamadou turned and saw me.

He didn't say anything. We never talked about it. He knew and understood.

I'm crying even as I write these words today. But I was not ashamed of my tears then, and I'm not ashamed now as I recall my experiences and emotions. Who knows, maybe I'll always cry whenever I remember this trip.

DAKAR AND THE GRIOT

We returned to Dakar via a dilapidated tugboat of a bus overflowing with people and livestock. After hours of being jostled about, almost violently at times, as the overburdened vehicle creaked and groaned along the rutted red roads, Mamadou and I arrived back at Ouagou Niayes Two.

We were both exhausted. Though it was early afternoon, we quickly washed and retired to our rooms to sleep. I would be leaving for Mauritania in a few days. There were still many questions I wanted to asked Mamadou before I left. For the moment, however, at least for several hours, we both needed our rest.

I closed the door behind me and was happy for the quiet and privacy of my little room. I shooed away the waterbugs who had taken up residence on my bed during my absence, chasing them out under the door. I covered myself with insect repellent and headed for the bed. When I pulled back the blanket, I saw another member of my personal welcoming party: a small tick making his way across my pillow. I dispatched him with a flick and lay down. I was soon out like a light.

※　　※　　※

When I awoke, it was evening. The air was cooling, and children were busy playing in the streets, running from one house to another. The communal dining room was filled with men, refugees who had travelled from the camps to Dakar to eat and sleep in the home of my hosts for a few days before they returned to the camps.

A bountiful dinner had been prepared. A savory meal of vegetables, rice, and fish, followed by the strong freshly brewed tea called ataye. Needless to say, Mamadou and I ate greedily and with gratitude.

Afterwards, the discussion turned naturally to Mauritania and the present conditions there. I saw this as my opportunity to ask Mamadou how the slavery system operated in his nation, and how it came to be. He began by explaining that slavery had been in Mauritania for centuries, and that the Africans there have known it in two forms. Not only were they fodder for the trans-Atlantic slave trade wrought by Europeans and Americans from the fifteenth to seventeen centuries, he said. They also suffered the earlier insult of being enslaved by the Arab invaders—then called "white Moors"—with whom they came into contact many hundreds of years prior. When the French colonized northwestern Africa in the last decade of the nineteenth century, Mamadou explained, they condoned the existing system of slavery and abetted the Arab slaveholders to the detriment of the native blacks.

"It is important to understand that in Mauritania you have two distinct communities," he continued. "There are the white Arabs and Berbers who live in the north and the black people who live in the south near the Senegal River. The blacks live in a stable environment. They have their animals and cattle. They are a sedentary people. The Arabs are nomadic people, traveling from place to place, so you already have a difference in mentality between the two communities."

"Sedentary people, because they want to live in a stable environment, are naturally passive people, people who want to live in peace instead of war and its problems. Nomadic people have to deal with traveling, aggression, and problems, and they tend to be more violent. Even when the blacks fight the Moor and win the war, they do not capture the Moor as slaves. They actually just fight them to defend themselves. However, because of the nature of nomadic people, the Moors tended to not only attack black villages and black people in the past, but when they fight them, they tend to capture people. And they tend to capture people as slaves because they need a work force. The Arabs have a different mentality and different objectives in life."

I asked Mamadou about the slave raids I had read and been told about, the raids in which Africans were kidnapped and tortured en masse. He explained it to me thusly: "The practice of going against a village and capturing people, kids and everything, and taking them away as slaves truly stopped in 1960 at independence. However, up to today, it is not on a large scale, but we still have kids, black kids, who have disappeared and who are found hundred of miles away as slaves."

"How do the Arabs capture black children and turn them into slaves?" I asked. His reply stunned me.

"There is something you can still observe very frequently in Mauritania," he said. "Some white Arabs go traveling about like normal people around cities and villages, and when they see black kids alone playing outside the village, they generally capture those kids. They are traveling

Mamadou distributing books at refugee camp

with their camels, you know, so they have a big basket. They put the child in the basket, close the basket, and then they run away with the child in the basket."

He sighed deeply, "And they still do that in 1995."

◈   ◈   ◈

I next asked Mamadou if suffering oppression and slavery at the hands of Arabs who worshipped Islam just as he did ever made him doubt his faith or experience conflicts with it. At first, he leaned back in his chair and smiled. Then he leaned forward and quite seriously stated, "I think we need to distinguish two things. Islam as a religion is almost perfect to me because it defends and promotes social justice and solidarity between people. The other thing that we need to take a look at separately is the fact that the Arab people are a separate group."

"When Islam came, it found that group, the Arab people, and they were already practicing slavery. They are a people who have always believed in slavery. So we have to make a difference between Islam as a religion practiced by Arabs and Arab traditions that have nothing to do with Islam because Islam is against slavery. We want our African-American brothers and sisters to understand that the Arabs as a community are intrinsically and fundamentally advocates of slavery. They believe in slavery, and they see in every black person a potential slave."

"When you, as a black person," he continued, "even though you are an African-American, when you visit Mauritania, you will experience directly what I am saying because young Mauritanian Arabs will treat you as they treat the black people who are taking care of them at home right now being their slaves, being anything the Arabs want them to be. Those Arab kids grow up with those slaves and believe that all black people must be like those people, that blacks should be for their service and do anything they want. They'll show you exactly what Arabs think about black people."

"If you remember, I told you in our first discussion that when I was arrested in 1986, the first thing they did was to put me in a room with four young Arabs who could be my kids. Those children told me, 'You see, you are a dirty black slave, and now you are now in revolt because you believe in freedom. What is your problem?'"

Mamadou sat back again and sighed heavily. "Still, I want to make clear that I am not accusing all Arabs. Perhaps some Arabs have cleaned their minds and their hearts. Maybe they feel differently now, but for most of them it is in their fundamental basic belief system that black people are slaves, period!

I nodded and he kept talking. "When you get to Mauritania, Samba

Kane, just open your eyes and observe. What you will see, for sure, is that when you go to the big houses belonging to the bourgeois Arabs or the big people of the Arab community, you will see something very noticeable: The black people who live in their houses—and there are almost sure to be a group of ten, maybe twenty of them—and the only thing they do is take orders! 'Go buy this! Go cook this! Clean the house!' And they will jump up and do it!"

"The way I see slavery in Mauritania today is like this: A slave is somebody who has no salary, who is not paid for his effort or his job. Who has no freedom to go or to leave the house. He lives in that house. He belongs to that person, and he does what the person wants him to do from morning to evening! Slaves have no freedom of movement. They have no salary, and they work twenty-four hours a day!"

Mamadou was becoming increasingly agitated as he spoke. "And these people do not sleep in rooms! There are no rooms in the house where these people are supposed to sleep. They sleep in the garage! Where people put their cars! And even then they have only a small spot, and that is where they are made to spend the night! And there is no plan for them to eat with people, no! They must wait until the master has finished eating, and the remains—the leftovers—that is what they give them to eat!"

"And this is only in the *city*!" he almost shouted. "If you have a chance to go into the countryside, you have in the black Mauritanian community what they call the Haratines. One part of them is what they call freed slaves, slaves who have gotten their freedom but who still live with their masters with the status of freed slaves. You also have the Abid," he said this later name with something next to disgust in his voice, "Abid are slaves, period! And they live their reality as slaves, period!"

I could tell that Mamadou was getting too worked up for a man who had just concluded such a long journey, and I tried to change the subject. But he had one more point to make.

"Samba Kane, in the countryside, you may have a chance to observe something that the Arabs there do. They treat their slave like *animals*! They do not allow weddings between their slaves. What they do is they select a strong black woman, and they pair her up with a strong black male of their own choosing. And then they put them together to breed, like animals!"

"And after the children are born and raised up a little," he almost spat out his words, "the Arab will sell the man and the woman to different masters, and they will never see each other again!"

SLAVERY IN SENEGAL

My work in Senegal had a twofold purpose: first, to interview Mauri-

tanian refugees and learn firsthand about their experiences at the hands of
their Arab Muslim countrymen and rulers, and second, to examine slave activity on the Senegalese side of the river. I had accomplished the first task
during my visits to the camps in Boki-Diawe', Wourossogui, and
Horkadiere. It was time to focus on the second.

Several of the people I spoke to at the refugee camps mentioned that
they had heard of slaves being taken to Dakar where they worked long days
and nights for their Beydane masters. Upon my return to the city, I asked
Bocar and Omar Ba if they could point out some of these slaves to me so I
could photograph and interview them. To my surprise, they matter-of-fact-
ly informed me that just down the street from the house where I was staying lived a white Moor who kept a whole houseful of slaves. They promised
to take me there whenever I wanted to go.

We waited one day until the Moor, who drove a shiny new BMW, left
the house. We approached the door and knocked. It was cautiously answered by two young girls about eleven or twelve years of age and a young
boy. The younger-looking of the two girls and the boy appeared to be a mixture of African and Arab. The older girl appeared to be pure black African.

Omar served as the interviewer, speaking in Wolof. I did the video-
taping. At first, the children showed great curiosity about the camera.
Omar asked the boy if there were any other slaves in the household. He
disappeared from sight for a moment and returned with an older man of
about sixty.

The old man was bald, and his skin was black and smooth. He looked
like he could be my grandfather. As he approached the doorway, he covered
his head with his turban. His eyes darted up and down the street to make
sure his master was not approaching. Interacting with free people was for-
bidden and punishable by a beating.

The old man told us that he was from Mauritania but had been in
Dakar for a long time. He identified the man he worked for as an Arab
sherif or religious leader. He indicated that he was the sherif's slave by stating that he was not paid for his work.

Sensing something out of the ordinary by the way the old man was talking to us so openly, one of the slave children ran to get another of the male
slaves who was in the house. This young man rushed up and stood between
Omar, the old man, and me with the video camera. He began berating the
elder man viciously, scolding him and warning that he should not be speaking to outsiders, that doing so would bring trouble upon himself and the
others. The young slave then told us to leave. We quickly terminated the interview and left the home.

Outside, I recalled an interview I had read in a Human Rights

Watch/Africa report prior to coming to Africa. In it, a man named Moustapha, a Mauritanian shepherd who escaped from his master in March 1990, made the following claims:

> If the master suspects that you are visiting free blacks, severe punishments await you. The first time I heard of the abolition, I was indifferent because I did not believe it. Then I began thinking about it and I became more curious. I returned to the same Hal-Pulaar neighbors to seek an explanation. My master became suspicious when I came back late and he found out that I had seen our Hal-Pulaar neighbors. In order to show his displeasure, I was undressed, my hands and feet tied up, and I was made to lie flat on my stomach in the burning sun. I was then whipped with a whip made of cowhide, and during the night, when the temperature was cold, they kept pouring water all over my body.[2]

I was thinking about Moustapha's comments as Omar, Bocar, and I walked hurriedly away from the Moor's house. I was moved that a man who was not free, who knew that he would probably be beaten for his boldness, would even try to communicate with us. The experience brought home for me, firsthand, an important realization: that the Africans from whom I would be receiving my information could find themselves in serious trouble.

In the days following that aborted interview, I would awaken in the early morning hours to stand by the gate and watch my Arab neighbor coming from the market with his slaves, the old man among them. I just couldn't believe it. How could this be going on in Senegal—a black country with a black leadership? I put this question to Mamadou, and the answer he gave me was tragic.

AFRICA'S SILENCE

In response to my question, Mamadou quoted Boubacar Joseph Ndiaye, the principal curator of Senegal's Gorée Island, the site of a sobering memorial to the countless enslaved Africans who were warehoused there prior to being shipped off to the Americas. As Ndiaye once said, Mamadou recalled, "I regret that for us Africans, [the] white slave traders [are] anonymous, but what I find more difficult to understand is...the role of African middlemen in this."[3]

Mamadou continued, pulling on his beard, as was his custom, and taking a deep, heavy breath: "The Pan-African Congress was held here in Dakar in 1994, and we of FLAM were not permitted to approach the delegates on the subject of slavery and apartheid. We were told that if we did, we would not be allowed to continue to operate in Senegal." Ostensibly, he claimed, there was an agreement between Mauritania and predominantly Muslim Senegal for Senegal to remain silent and cover up the mistreatment and enslavement of black Mauritanians.

I asked Mamadou how he felt, not only about the silence of Senegal and other African countries on this issue, but about their willingness to suppress information about it.

"I think this is a problem that the African community has—about many issues, not only slavery—but several other issues," he replied. "Africans tend to tell you, 'I don't want to interfere with a country's or a nation's internal problems. I will mind my own business.' To me, it is just a way of running away from their responsibilities. I don't think it is a responsible way to deal with such important issues."

"Fundamentally, black people have internal problems," he continued. "They do not act together, and the best proof of this is that a hundred thousand black Mauritanians have been expelled from Mauritanian to Senegal and Mali. That is where they live now, and they want to go home. The other African countries do not mention that particular issue, and they do not deal with it."

Mamadou could sense my mounting discomfort, but he pressed on. "A most shocking thing happened recently. When forty-two Palestinians were expelled from their country, an Islamic conference was held in Dakar. All of the African delegates came together to propose a resolution to get those forty-two Palestinians back home, but not one mentioned the sixty thousand black Mauritanians who are living as refugees in Senegal! That was a very shocking thing to see how these Africans were so concerned about those Palestinians. Now, don't get me wrong, I too support the Palestinians. They are our brothers, and I agree that they deserved to go back home. But I and my other brothers and sisters, the tens and hundreds of thousands who were expelled from Mauritania also deserve to go back home!"

"Overall," he said, sighing, "African people give you the impression that they do not care about what is happening to their brothers and sisters right under their own noses. They do not put the right issues on their agenda, issues that are important for black people!"

"It is important to understand, Samba Kane, that African societies have been the victim of so many things in the past. Colonization has destroyed so much of the social structure of African societies. All those who say that Africans are in solidarity and that Africans care so much for each other simply don't have the power to act on situations and change them! Africans are concerned about surviving on a daily basis and finding enough food to eat! Many African people are so messed up today, that you cannot expect them to take strong action about such issues. Lack of courage, property, and everything else can explain why African people are acting like they are acting today!"

Mamadou shifted his weight, and a look of sadness settled on his face. "Besides," he concluded, "I don't believe those Africans were even very sincere when they put that resolution for the Palestinians on the table. You know the diplomatic pressure and ways that Arab countries can lobby African countries!"

I asked Mamadou to go into greater detail about this last point. He jumped up to continue: "Samba Kane, the Arabs give us money! If an African nation or nations present a resolution on Palestine to the United Nations or at a conference, the Arabs promise lots of aid in return. Next thing you know, you're receiving money from Kuwait or Saudi Arabia! So, on one hand, it is a strategy to get money. But on the other hand, it is proof that our people have really been hit hard in terms of their courage, personality, and awareness of what is right and what is wrong being taken away from them."

"And here is the crux of it all, Samba Kane: Mauritania is actually *protected* by those Arab countries that meet with Africans in the Islamic conferences! Those countries, those Arab countries, will never agree to condemn Mauritania or to take action against it for its slavery activities!"

Abdoulaye Sy stepped up behind us and joined Mamadou and me at the gate. "I overheard you two talking," he said in broken English. "I think that Mamadou spoke very well about all the issues, and I would just like to add one little thing. Our leaders, our heads of state, are *all* dependent on international aid. They are all cowards! They say: 'Mind your own business at home and I will mind my own business at home, and everything will be fine.' That is the reason why all the black heads of state who were in Dakar were silent about Mauritania!"

Abdoulaye went on to incriminate the French neocolonialists for their role in the matter. When former French president Mitterand was in power, he explained, Mitterand gave specific instructions to the Francophone African leaders to "just be quiet" about the Mauritanian issue. It happened that Mitterand's son, Christian, was living in Mauritania at the time and working there as a newspaper reporter. Christian Mitterand was a very, very close friend of Mauritanian president Maaouya Ould Sid Ahmed Taya. He asked his father to be supportive of Taya, and Mitterand complied. And it was France, Abdoulaye reminded me, that had earlier cut Senegal into two pieces, placed the Arabs with their slaves and free Africans in the new territory called Mauritania, and given full power to the Arabs.

The realities of the situation began to take shape in my mind. Black Africa was still under subjugation, not only to corrupt black leaders but also to Arab and French manipulation and influence. The African homeland

I was experiencing for the first time was not free physically, economically, psychologically, or spiritually. It was an emasculated child suffocating under layers of external domination.

In my head, I was putting together a picture. That picture included the inability of the leaders of today's African nations to show concern for their fellow Africans who are still in slavery. It also included a picture of their willingness to work with contemporary slaveholders and slavetraders to suppress information about the atrocities that are still going on, on African soil. However, a key image in the picture I was forming was the disintegration of African society due to both the trans-Atlantic slave trade and the sub-Saharan slave trade. Add to this decades of Arab occupation, European colonialism, and neocolonialism, and you have the context for slavery to persist and flourish in the midst of what appear to be free African nations.

My visit to Senegal had served me well as a base for my preparations to make the trip to Mauritania. I was ready to continue my journey. It was time to do what I had come to Africa to do.

Phase Two

On January 2, 1996, after obtaining my visa in Dakar, I bid farewell to Mamadou Ba and boarded a flight to Mauritania. I was alone again, and nervous. Once again, I would be going into strange territory without knowing the people I would be staying with. The night before, I had learned, the person who was supposed to be my contact in Mauritania had become fearful and backed out of the task. A new contact had been found at the last minute.

That morning, as I was finishing up my packing I wondered who my new guide would be and if he or she would have the courage to risk supporting me and my research. Then I worried: Suppose the people in Mauritania are not of the same dedicated spirit and mind as Mamadou? What did it mean that one guide had already lost heart? Then again, had that person gone to the authorities and told them I was coming? Should I risk taking this trip, given these conditions?

I didn't have answers to any of my questions, so I decided to swallow my fear and devote all of my energies to packing and getting ready. Afterwards, I sat in my room, looking at my luggage until Mamadou came to tell me it was time to go to the airport. Omar and Bocar stopped at the doorway of the room and made small talk. I could tell they were just as nervous and worried as I was. Mamadou returned with a taxi, and we were on our way to the airport.

I was very, very quiet during the ride. Quite frankly, I was scared. Mamadou sensed my anxiety and tried to make jokes about it. He succeeded in making me laugh and feel a bit better. I had come this far, I realized, and there was no turning back. From that point on, I concentrated on one thought: If there was a higher power concerned about the life of people who are oppressed and enslaved, I said to myself, then this power would successfully guide my journey.

❋   ❋   ❋

My plane was bound for Nouakchott, the desert capital of Mauritania. Nouakchott is a city with a high concentration of freed slaves or Haratines, runaway slaves, slaves, and Negro-Africans or those blacks who had never been enslaved. It is also a city with a fair amount of political activity. Two important anti-slavery organizations have their headquarters there: El Hor and SOS-Esclaves.

This sun-blasted setting is also where a thousand blacks were massacred in a border dispute between Mauritania and Senegal that began on April 9, 1989. As a result of that dispute, riots and attacks on Mauritanian boutiques began in Dakar, and several white Moors were killed. Two weeks later, on April 24, anti-Senegalese riots erupted in Nouakchott and Nouadhibou, resulting in the deaths of over a thousand more blacks, most of whom were killed in Nouakchott.

My objective was to live with an African family in Nouakchott and blend into the Mauritanian community without being monitored by the authorities. I had no official authorization to conduct my research, and if I was discovered, I would at the very least be in serious trouble with the Arab-run government. At the worst, who knew what would happen?

I must have been lost in such thoughts during the entire fifty-minute flight because the next thing I knew, I heard the voice of the captain announcing our arrival. The information panel overhead signaled red: "Fasten Your Seatbelts." We were making our approach.

CHAPTER SIX

Every colonized people, in other words, every people in whose soul an inferiority complex has been created by the death and burial of its local cultural originality—finds itself face to face with the language of the civilizing nation; that is, with the culture of the mother country. The colonized is elevated above his jungle status in proportion to his adoption of the mother country's cultural standards. He becomes whiter as he renounces his blackness, his jungle.[1]
—FRANTZ FANON

The jet lands smoothly on the runway, touching down almost imperceptibly. It is late in the evening and the sky is darkening quickly, but I turn and look out the window at Mauritania, the African nation I have been researching, reading, writing, and talking about so intensely for the past eighteen months. As the airliner begins to taxi toward the Nouakchott Airport terminal, I unfasten my seat belt, stand, and begin pulling my bags down from the overhead luggage compartment. Soon I am in the aisle standing among the other passengers, jostling for position to leave the aircraft.

Funny. I had not noticed them before. The other passengers, that is. I guess I had been in such deep thought throughout the flight that I had become oblivious to anything or anyone else. I notice them now, however. They are a mixture of Africans, Arabs, and whites.

Oddly enough, as I walk toward the aircraft door, I am totally unafraid. If anything, I exude an air of defiance. I'm not sure if my bravado is an attempt to mask my anxieties or simply a reflection of my anger about the many atrocities I had heard and read so much about—the countless un-speakable crimes that have been committed against the black people in this country. In any event, defiance was in my manner and in my bearing as I stepped off the plane into the evening air.

◈　◈　◈

I must have been thinking about Emmett Till, the northern black Amer-ican teenager who travelled down South in the 1950s, the garrulous young boy who had made up his mind that no one was going to call him a nigger. Or maybe I was thinking of Richard Pryor, who, in one of his early movies, was depicting an innocent brother who had been sent to prison, and who, upon walking into the jail cell packed with hardened criminals, im-mediately "jumped bad" and started "pimpin'"—you know, be-bopping and taking those long, hard strides—and shouting, "Yeah, I'm bad! I'm BAdddDDDDD!!"

I hope I wasn't be-bopping as I walked into the terminal, but I was probably pretty close to it. I knew that my black skin labeled me as a po-tential slave in this strange desert land, and I was instinctively striving to maintain a proud self-image. Of course, I knew my attitude alone couldn't protect me from the Mauritanian authorities. According to several of the re-ports I had read prior to my trip, they had already killed thousands of black people. Still, I was intent on sending a message to everyone around me that *I* was not a slave. *I* was not inferior, and nobody had better not *try* treating me that way!

◈　◈　◈

Immediately after passing through the first gate, I was approached by my Mauritanian contact, a pleasant and likeable fellow whom I will call "Mr. B." to protect his identity. Mr. B. spoke passable English. He told me that I had been easy to recognize because Mamadou had informed him that I would be wearing a red baseball cap. He introduced himself while gather-ing up my suitcases, then ordered me to follow him to the customs desk.

After being processed through customs, I followed Mr. B. to the termi-nal to pick up the rest of my luggage. As we waited for the bags to arrive, I studied the activities and the people around me for the first time. In those few brief moments, I learned some very important things about the African nation I was visiting.

The first was that if you go to Mauritania expecting the twin devils of racism and slavery to jump out in front of you into plain sight, you will be either relieved or disappointed, depending on your point of view. Mau-ritania is a study in subtlety. What's going there is difficult to detect.

The capital city of Nouakchott, for example, has a clean, quiet airport. All passengers seem to be processed equitably and efficiently without regard to race or color. The security personnel seem pleasant and courteous to all. There are no overt signs to indicate that this is in any way an unpleasant place.

Yet, if one observes more closely, looks just a little deeper, the problem of the color line in Mauritania becomes immediately apparent. Most apparent to me, as I stood waiting in the airport, was the fact that all of the high-ranking personnel I saw were Arabs or Haratines, while all those in the low-ranking positions—the porters, baggage handlers, and cleaners—were Negro-Africans.

My luggage arrived and we hurried from the terminal without incident. Outside, we were greeted by two men who had been waiting patiently to meet me. Mr. B. told me that one of the men was related to one of my Mauritanian friends in the United States. He explained that we would be staying in the home of this man and his family during my stay in Nouakchott. The men took my bags and led us to a waiting car.

◈　　◈　　◈

The night air was dry and warm as we climbed into the car and struck out for the city. As we rode, we began to talk. Both of the men spoke some English. My host asked how my friend, his relative, was doing. He told me that he hoped I had a big appetite because his family had prepared a huge dinner for me. They had also prepared a nice place for me to sleep, he claimed.

Mr. B. and I talked about other people we both knew. "Tonight, however, you relax," he said. "Tomorrow we can discuss how to make the necessary contacts for your research."

I did begin to relax a bit after that. I could just feel that my new contacts were good people who were very supportive of my mission.

◈　　◈　　◈

The car took a circular route into town, and despite the darkness, I tried to take in as much as I could of the beleaguered country I had studied so intensely.

My first impressions were that I had travelled back in time. My God, I thought, this city is a study in penury! Indeed, the poverty of the Mauritanian nation as a whole is reflected in its capital city's almost complete lack of infrastructure. There are few paved streets or sidewalks to talk of in Nouakchott, but many, many trash-strewn dirt roads throughout, giving the city a bombed-out, desolate appearance.

Conditions were somewhat better in the central business section, but not by much. There, we saw a few Arabs and Africans in western and traditional dress moving about in the shadows, but for the most part, the streets were virtually empty. The silence of the city, broken occasionally by the sound of a donkey-drawn flatbed cart or an ancient, sputtering taxi, was almost eerie.

Once off the streets and in the home of my hosts, everything changed. For security reasons, I cannot describe the people I met or the place where I stayed in any great detail. I can tell you, however, that my hosts and aides accepted me as if I was a member of their own families, and they tried to make me very comfortable during my stay.

Their home was clean and cozy. Mr. B and I shared a room, one with a real bed with legs that raised it off the floor. Mr. B. insisted that, as a guest, I sleep in the bed while he slept on a mattress placed on the floor. I thanked him and turned to look at that bed with its wonderful clean sheets. No bugs or ticks here, I said to myself, remembering my nighttime experiences in Senegal. I could not wait to bathe and jump into it!

There was a trade-off, though. In Senegal, I may have had to contend with all kinds of insects in my room at night, but I at least had a toilet where I could sit and do my business. In my new Mauritanian quarters, my toilet was two bricks straddling a hole in a secluded courtyard. You had to either stand or squat down on those bricks and aim for the hole, which was only about four inches in diameter. Still, the trade-off was alright with me. I was so happy to be able to sleep free of bugs that having to improve my aim seemed a minor matter.

❋   ❋   ❋

I awoke in the morning feeling rested and refreshed. I stepped out of my room into the cool morning air, stood on my two bricks, and fired away, right on target. After breakfast, I met with Mr. B to discuss my plans. We decided that I should send for an interpreter right away. Mr. B contacted a woman who had agreed earlier to serve in this capacity.

While waiting for the interpreter to come, I spent some time getting to know my host and his family. They often met in the large family room to talk and eat or sit. This was also where the family's prized television set was located. I spent many hours whiling away the time in front of their t.v., learning about the strange land I was visiting.

❋   ❋   ❋

My exposure to the Mauritanian media helped me to fully understand the deadly power of subtle racism. Mauritania has one state-run radio station and one television station. Programs in African languages or about African culture are barred from the radio during the hours when radio transmissions travel the farthest—from eight o'clock in the evening to six in the morning. Mauritanian television permits only two hours and five minutes of government-monitored African-language programming in any week. On Mondays and Thursdays, it runs twenty-five minutes of programming in Haal-pulaar'en, the language of the Fulani. On Tuesdays and Fridays, twenty-five minutes are set aside for programs in Sonin'ke. Sundays are for Wolof, but again, just twenty-five minutes. And this is compared to twenty-five hours of programming in Arabic and four-and-a-half hours in French.[2]

Thus, except for an occasional television broadcast from Senegal, virtually all the images on Mauritanian television are Arab or white. Black Mauritanians are all but invisible. This same invisibility, I learned, applies to almost every aspect of the national image, from its advertising and tourist literature, to its museums and market places.

African men are especially minimized in this regard. As my host explained, the possibility for employment for Negro-African men in Mauritania was extremely dim because all of the businesses of substance are owned and operated by Arabs. There had once been a number of black businesses, he said, but they had been destroyed during the 1989 massacres. Since then, many black men had left to study abroad, only to return and find nothing for them to do—no work above menial tasks, that is—once they received their degrees. Even if a black Mauritanian did get a job working for an Arab, my host told me, he would be replaced as soon as one of his employer's relatives needed a position.

◈　　◈　　◈

The racism to be found in Mauritania is not readily apparent to most visitors because the Mauritanian Arab interacts with blacks far differently than does the white man of the American South or the Boer of South Africa. Unlike the United States of just a few decades ago, Mauritania has no overtly racially discriminatory laws. Blacks and whites are not forced to attend separate schools or live in separate neighborhoods. And unlike black South Africans of just a few years ago, Mauritanian Africans do not need passbooks. Interracial marriage is not illegal, and everyone can vote.

So, what is the problem?

The problem is that Mauritania's Arabs sincerely believe that blacks are inferior and are born to be slaves. They believe that a black man, woman, or child's place in life is to serve an Arab master, and it does not matter to them whether that black is a Christian or a fellow Muslim. The Arabs don't believe that they have to make any laws to stop interracial marriage because they think it's a disgrace for an Arab to marry a black person, anyway. Historically, the autocratic Beydane-run government has never really bothered to create any laws, except for cosmetic reasons. Arab cultural attitudes and beliefs that support slavery and deny equal access to black Africans are the *real* law.

Yet, oddly enough, the Mauritanian Arab does not seem to mind living in the same neighborhood or community with black Africans. He does not even seem to mind if a black person or two is appointed to a government position, because everyone in the country knows those blacks are only tokens, controlled by their Arab patrons. Those who do gain access have usually had their cultural wiring ripped out to the extent that they become self-hating non-entities who do their people more harm than good.

And so what if black Mauritanians can vote? The elections are always rigged to ensure that black Africans cannot gain any real power or change their status in society. And any black who poses a real threat to the government always seems to disappear quickly and quietly from the scene.

Subsequently, visitors to Mauritania typically experience none of the underside of this nation's silent terror. They experience only the pleasant and polite Arab, the smiling white Muslim face welcoming them to "his" country. And that Arab, knowing how badly American blacks, especially black Muslims, want to be accepted, will call his black American visitor "brother"—even though he himself owns several black men who look just like the brother and fully supports a system that is hell-bent on denying every black African in sight his or her freedom!

That is why I say anyone, white or black, who tries to understand the Mauritanian experience by viewing it through lenses fashioned by Western experience is going to miss what is going on there. Mauritania's free blacks are in a daily struggle for their lives, their livelihoods, their self-esteem, and their dignity. I felt it more and more every day I was there, and I struggled against it along with my host family, their friends, and relatives. Like them, I had to keep reaching for reasons to hold my head up, to be proud, to survive.

❋   ❋   ❋

These are the kinds of things I learned living among the Negro-Africans of Nouakchott. I would never have learned these things stay-ing in a cushy hotel located in the business district as a guest of the Mauritanian government. No self-respecting black Mauritanian would have said a word to me if they had even suspected I was working with or had the support of the Arab-run government. For them, too much is at stake. These people put their lives on the line when they work with outsiders who are trying to tell the world what is really happening in their country. They are also the ones who must live in fear of that fateful knock on the door in the middle of the night, after the journalists have come and gone.

That is why it was so important to me to live among them, these blacks. To feel what they feel daily, to wake up and eat out of the same communal bowl with them, to sit with them and feel time stop because there is nothing to do. Nothing. And no where to go. To languish, day after day, frying in the heat of the African sun, and feel that awful racist funk settle over my spirit like stagnant water.

I experienced what they experienced because I wanted to know the truth, and because I wanted my brothers and sisters in Mauritania to know that there was at least one black person from America who cared that black people on African soil were being oppressed and enslaved—and wanted to do something to help them even after the article had been written and the story published.

After a few days, it became clear that the interpreter had backed out. She kept promising to show up but she never did. I asked Mr. B if we could get someone else. He stated that there was another woman who was very active in the Mauritanian anti-slavery movement who could be of help. Her name was Hapsa Dia, and he sent word to her immediately asking for her help. Hapsa Dia agreed, and we left after dinner for a meeting with her.

Hapsa Dia turned out to be one of the most courageous women I have ever met. A petite and demure Negro-African woman, she greeted us warmly and both her composure and her command of the English language made me instantly comfortable. When we were all seated, she asked me to explain my mission in Mauritania and what I expected from the people there.

I explained that I was a journalist and the director of an anti-slavery organization in the United States who had come to determine if the charges that slavery existed in Mauritania were true. I told her that African-Americans were becoming increasingly aware of the situation in her country and were interested in mobilizing to address the issue but that they needed sound documentation of the extent of the problem.

Hapsa Dia sat there intently listening to me, absorbing everything I was saying. Then all of a sudden she started to cry. Shocked, and worried that I had said something to offend her, I turned to Mr. B. and the rest of my party for help. They said nothing. I asked Hapsa Dia what was wrong.

She said, "This is a very important moment for me, Mr. Sam. I am so very happy to know that our African-American brothers want to know about all that is happening here. I have read much about African-Americans and how they fought for their freedom. I have read about the civil rights movement and your people's courage. Your coming here to Mauritania is a sign! I believe that the African-Americans can help us, that they can show us how we in Mauritania can also get our freedom! So please, excuse my tears, but I am feeling very happy and emotional at this moment."

My heart went out to her. I told her that I wanted to take everything that she and the others could teach me about Mauritania back to America so that I could help the anti-slavery movement throw its support behind the fight to end the practice of slavery and the human rights abuses that the Negro-Africans in her country were suffering.

We went on to work out the details of my trip. She told me that there were several people it was important for me to meet. We decided to set out early the next morning and travel all over the city so that she could point out to me both the subtleties and the brutal realities of Mauritania's peculiar system of slavery.

◈   ◈   ◈

After returning to my hosts' home from my meeting with Hapsa Dia, I had dinner with the family. Later, I bid them good night and went to fetch the buckets of water I would need for my shower. After showering, I lay down in my bed under the mosquito net and contemplated the work ahead.

That evening, as I drifted off to sleep under the balmy, starlit African sky, I realized many things. First, I realized that African-Americans are role models for many people throughout the world. In Mauritania, African-Americans are highly respected and their help greatly desired. Indeed, many of the black Africans I had met believed that once African-Americans knew what was going on, they could help abolish slavery in Mauritania and in other parts of northwestern Africa in much the same way they helped destroy apartheid in South Africa.

I realized as well that we Africans who have survived the terrors of the New World have a critical role to play in the ongoing liberation of Africa. It was not going to be easy, I knew, because we blacks in the U.S. are still under quite a bit of pressure ourselves. Yet there is no way we can turn our backs on our African kin who are still suffering from that which we have suffered and borne with our blood, sweat, and tears. No, it would not be easy. But it would be the beginning of our spiritual liberation and the beginning of the end of slavery once and for all.

◈   ◈   ◈

The next day I awoke and went immediately to Hapsa Dia's house. I asked her how we should begin conducting our research. She responded, "Today I will take you to the Fifth Market, where people are living even now under the yoke of slavery and working at the mercies of their masters."

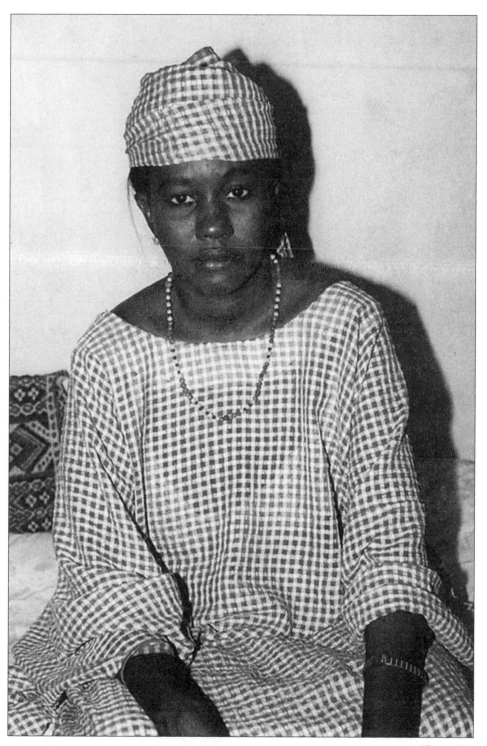

Hapsa Dia

When we reached the market, Hapsa Dia began pointing out several blacks whom she identified as slaves. I asked her how she could identify slaves from non-slaves. I remembered how it was done in Senegal and I wondered if the approach was consistent. As Hapsa Dia informed me, "It is like the difference between the European and the Arab people. These slaves are black men, but what differentiates them from the Negro-African is that they are culturally different. Their cultural behavior is not the same. For example, the slaves, you will notice, speak Hassaniya [the Arab dialect of Mauritania] as opposed to Hal-Pulaar or other languages of the Negro-African. And they live with their masters."

I was very curious about this last remark. How did she know that most of the blacks we saw in the marketplace were slaves living with their masters? To this, Hapsa Dia replied, "Because I know that these white Arabs do not have black friends! Plus, Mauritania is not a big country. We all know that is going on here in Nouakchott. I was born in this country, and I know how things are. Still, even though slavery is an established fact in Mauritania, it would be very difficult for me to ask of a black man, 'Are you a slave?' because it is like an insult."

"Is there any question that you could ask these people that would not be insulting?" I asked.

"Well," she replied, "I could ask them, for example, 'Are you paid for your work?' This is important because there are rarely any written contracts, and many masters try to pass off their slaves as domestics or family members who receive no financial remuneration. But when a black person responds that he or she is not paid for their labor, it is a strong indicator that you are speaking to a person in bondage."

"Then there are other indicators. You could ask whether or not the black children of both sexes and of all ages who live in these Arab households are going to school. This is important because slaves are rarely given any education, nor do they receive medical treatment."

Hapsa Dia told me that Negro-Africans in Mauritania can clearly identify the slaves in their society that would be invisible to researchers and journalists from the outside, who neither understand nor are familiar with their culture. That is why, she added, the Negro-Africans say that you can walk through Mauritania and see slaves everywhere and nowhere.

I too would achieve a similar awareness in the days ahead as I observed black men in the marketplace and elsewhere in Nouakchott. I saw them doing all manner of work throughout the city: racing about to keep their masters' teacups full, carrying unbearably heavy loads from place to place while Arab overseers lolled about or shouted out orders. I saw them chauffeuring Arab businessmen around town and working from sunup to sun-

A white moor giving orders to his slave to make the rice bags ready to be shipped across from Rosso Senegal over to Mauritania. Afterwards, he goes to prepare his ablution for the Muslim prayer, perhaps in the hope that God will keep the status quo. The slave is not required to pray if the master needs his sweat.

down in the date fields of those who owned both the fields and the people who labored in them.

I wondered what it would feel like if, in New York City where I lived, I had to watch blacks serve whites in the same kinds of ways. I wondered if I could remain silent as I saw black women being sold or rented out or black children being taken from their parents and sold, never to see their mothers or fathers or sisters or brothers again. I didn't think I could. Why then, was it viewed by so many as acceptable when it occurred in Mauritania?

In the days that followed, besides taking me all over the city, Hapsa Dia introduced me to a number of other courageous Negro-Africans whose efforts made it possible for me to accomplish what I had come to Mauritania to do. These people became my patient teachers, at great risk to themselves. I began to meet regularly with three Mauritanian activists: Ibrahima Sarr,

Abid woman (top). *Negro-African woman* (bottom)

Fara Ba, and Sitty Hai'dara, Fara's wife. The two men had both suffered persecution in the Oualata prison, the same hell-hole where my friend Mamadou Bocar Ba had been tortured. Ibrahima, Fara, and Sitty worked hard to arrange meetings for me with Haratine anti-slavery leaders and others who had escaped or been liberated from slavery.

❖   ❖   ❖

I need to explain here something about the relationship between the Negro-African and Haratine anti-slavery movements. The analogy of a lifeguard faced with the dilemma of swimming out into shark-infested waters to save a person's life best explains the dual tensions that the Negro-African abolitionists experience in their quest to stop the practice of slavery in Mauritania. Not only must the lifeguard protect himself from the sharks but also from those whom they want to save. In the feverish and desperate state of mind created by the condition of drowning, the flailing arms and legs of the endangered one can cause his or her potential rescuer to drown as well. Therefore, lifeguards approach drowning victims with caution.

Similarly, although Negro-Africans, or members of Mauritania's free black ethnic groups (specifically, the Hal-Pulaar), are steadfastly committed to the abolition of slavery in their country, the majority of Haratines active in the anti-slavery movement are nonetheless suspicious of them. They tend to concentrate on their own issues and often do not have at heart the interests of the Negro-Africans, who are also oppressed by the Arab-run government of Mauritania. Importantly, Haratine leaders of the Mauritanian anti-slavery movement expressly maintain that the purpose of their movement is to free *black* Arabs from enslavement by other *Arabs*.

There are vast cultural differences between the two groups as well. Like their slave counterparts, the Haratines are Arab-centered, whereas Negro-Africans tend to be African-centered. Negro-African women wear the traditional clothing and hairstyles of indigenous Africans. Haratine and Abid women wear veils and fabrics that reflect Arab culture. Negro-Africans have retained their language and culture, while the Haratines, as a result of their slavery experience, have lost almost every aspect of their African origin except their black skin color.

In addition, the Arab strategy of *"adhrab al abid bil abid,"* which means "hit the slave with the slave," has been successfully utilized by the Beydane ruling class to pit black against black in Mauritania. The Mauritanian government continues to use its predominantly Haratine military and police forces to murder, rape, oppress, and control Negro-African populations.

While in Mauritania I also discovered that several Haratine leaders believe that Negro-Africans practice slavery in the south of Mauritania just as the Arabs practice it in the north.[3] None of the interviews or research reports I had read prior to my trip, including those conducted by human rights organizations such as Human Rights Watch/Africa or the London-based Anti-Slavery International organization, had corroborated any such charges. Nor, to my knowledge, had any cases ever been produced, either by the Haratines or the Arab government (which would find it tactically expedient to fuel such charges), to document the buying or selling of other Africans by Negro-Africans.

Yet, one of my Negro-African contacts in Nouakchott shared with me a copy of a document entitled *20 Questions on Slavery in Mauritania*. This document, authored by Boubacar Messaoud, the devoted and courageous leader of the prominent Haratine anti-slavery organization, SOS-Esclaves, steadfastly asserts that chattel slavery is being practiced by Negro-Africans in northwestern Africa. In it, Messaoud states the following (emphasis mine):

Is slavery a racial problem in Mauritania?

Some people tend to believe so. Under the pretext that the ancient slaves in the Arab society were blacks, some people wanted to recover their cause by taking it for other situations. Slavery in Mauritania is not a social problem.

Slavery does exist in both Arab and black African societies. The Haratine who constitute the majority are Arabs and will remain faithful to their identity. The matters in dispute is of a social order and should remain so...

Does slavery exist in the black African community?

*Contrary to a received and widespread idea, **slavery does not exist in the Arab society only**. It is certainly more visible, because epidermically [it is] obvious, but, under the mask of the common color of the skin, it also survives among the black Africans. Be they Wolof, Peul or Sonin'ke, the latter has a house slavery which, somehow, is similar to the one practiced by their Arab compatriots.*[4]

Of course, when I read the above and heard the claims of the Haratine leaders myself, I immediately embarked on my own mini-investigation. As far as I was concerned, if the charges were true, then two societies, Arab and African, needed to be exposed and purged of their incivilities. If the charges were false, then they were detrimental to the anti-slavery movement because they not only diluted the force of that movement but also fostered divisions between Negro-Africans and Haratines.

I conducted numerous interviews on this topic while in Nouakchott. The Negro-Africans I spoke with ardently denied the presence of slaveholding among their group. There was something in their responses that disturbed me, however. Content analysis of my interviews revealed a reluctance on their part to explain why otherwise highly regarded, intelligent, and courageous Haratine anti-slavery leaders would make such charges. What then, I wondered, was the reason behind this reticence?

After many interviews, I discovered the answer to my question. The heart of the matter lay in the Negro-Africans' shame over the enduring presence of an indigenous caste system that continues to discriminate against black Africans whose families were, at one time long ago, the slaves of other Africans. According to Ibrahima Sarr and Hapsa Dia, this intraracial prejudice currently manifests as the unfair treatment Negro-Africans with slave histories receive from other Negro-Africans when competing for jobs and other opportunities. It can also damage the marriage prospects of an African who wants to marry outside of his or her caste.

I remembered a quote from a 1994 newspaper article I had read before coming to Mauritania. The article was by Associated Press writer Mark Fritz. It was titled, "Rights of Ownership: Slavery's Lingering Hold on Mauritania." In it, Fritz reported on an interview with a Ha-Pulaar human rights lawyer named Fatimata Mbaye, who had been imprisoned for six months in 1986 for her anti-slavery activity. Mbaye maintained, however, that while "the white people [Mauritanian Arabs] have slaves and the black people have slaves...the *Hal-Pulaar slave today is mostly a symbol, we can't buy or sell somebody.*"[5]

And that, realistically, is as far as the charge of slaveholding by the Negro-African community can go: it is a thing of the past. Yet, why do so many Haratine leaders continue to accuse their Negro-African countrymen of practicing slavery in the present day on the same scale as the Beydanes?

The reason, I believe, is that, despite the fact that they are viewed by the Arabs as *Abid* or slaves, regardless of their freed status, and also as inferior due to their race, most Haratines see themselves as Arabs *first*, not as Africans. They also hold fast to the identities given them by their Arab former masters, even though Arab society has relegated them to the bottom of the social ladder. As such, they are torn between the power their former masters have over their minds—a vestige of centuries of cultural assimilation—and their desire to end slavery amongst their people.

Having lost their African identity, the Haratines of Mauritania naturally seek to protect the only identity they have left: their Arab identity. Because they do not want Arabs to be viewed as radically different on the moral issue of slavery, they consequently charge that slavery exists among Negro-Africans as well. However, it is a charge that does not stand up to inspection. Worse, it is an instrument created to help Mauritania's "black

Arabs" reconcile and protect the pristine Arab image that has been affixed to their minds as a result of their slavery experiences.

Despite the tensions between the two groups, opposition to slavery is a prominent plank in the platform of every Negro-African opposition party in Mauritania, and most Negro-Africans show amazing sympathy for the plight of the Haratines. They also manifest a profound understanding of the effects of slavery on those they perceive as their brothers and sisters lost within an inherently evil system of mental, spiritual, and physical oppression. The two groups also manage to work together fairly extensively on the issue of abolishing slavery. As a result of this fragile coalition, my Negro-African contacts were able to arrange for me to meet and interview several Haratine anti-slavery leaders and runaway slaves who had come to them for protection.

Nevertheless, I gained the highest respect for the Haratine anti-slavery leaders I met during my trip. Their courage and determination are extraordinary. This is especially true of Boubacar Messaoud of SOS-Esclaves.

Born into slavery in the Mauritanian village of Rosso in 1945, Messaoud escaped by fleeing from his master's house when he was in his teens. Fortune smiled upon him, and as a young man, he was sent to study in Moscow, where he received a degree in architecture. Upon returning to his native land, he dedicated himself to the struggle against slavery and for the emancipation of his people. He was among a group of Haratines tried in court because of their involvement in the El Hor movement in 1980, before the pseudo-abolition of slavery by the Beydane government. However, he withdrew from El Hor in 1994 and the next year established SOS-Esclaves.

One of my first interviews was with Messaoud Ould Boulkheir, the sixty-three-year-old president of the underground anti-slavery organization El Hor. Before assuming leadership of this organization, Boulkheir served as Mauritania's Minister of Rural Development. He also ran for mayor of Nouakchott in 1990. However, unlike many Haratines who are chosen for government positions because they can be easily manipulated or because they seek the relative prestige and comfort these positions provide, the elegant, bearded Boulkheir is a man of solid character.

Boulkheir was born into a family taken as slaves; thus, he was considered a slave at birth. He explained to me that, in Mauritania, slave status is passed through one's mother, but a slave could become free in four ways:

First, you can refuse the condition of being a slave. Even if you sacrifice yourself, this is the best way to be free. In order to improve your condition, even if you lost your life, this is the price. The second way to be free is the problem of the master. If he wants to give freedom to his slaves, he can give it if he so desires.

Messaoud Ould Boulkheir

The third is by paying a sum of money to one's master. The fourth is by the law—to force the government to grant freedom to all people. As I am a victim of slavery, I think that the best way to be free is to join an organization such as El Hor. As the head of this organization, I think I can improve this situation. Some people do not have the courage to be in the organization and to talk about the condition. I am here to do it [since] I have had the chance to go to school and to become aware. Also, I am following the ex-

Jebada Mint Maouloud

ample of my mother, who rose up against her master to fight for her freedom because she was badly treated.

Boulkheir introduced me to a woman named Jebada Mint Maouloud. He explained that Jebada had been "emancipated" from slavery because her extensive injuries rendered her "unfit" for service. Her face was covered by a veil, and she kept her hands out of sight until Boulkheir asked her to show them to me. They were terribly disfigured. Through my interpreter, Hapsa Dia, I asked Jebada what had happened to her.

As she began telling her story, Jebada started to cry. Boulkheir explained that this happened whenever she talked about her experiences as a slave, even though it was years ago. She continued nonetheless.

When she was seven years old, Jebada made the mistake of allowing one of her master's animals to be eaten by a wild beast. For this, the Arab severely punished her by lashing her hands together tightly with a rope and hanging her from the center post of his tent for many days. Worse still, she was ordered to remain absolutely still while she was thus suspended or face further punishment.

When she was finally cut down from the post, Jebada's hands were horribly atrophied as a result of the rope having restricted the flow of blood to them for so long. Her master sent her to a healer who tried to save her

Jebada's hands

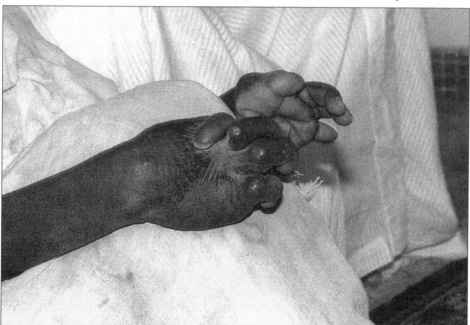

hands but "they had become very big and started to stink," she said. They got so bad, she told Hapsa, that everyone in her master's village would complain when the wind would change because they could smell her hands, which never healed properly. Having been rendered useless, Jebada was expelled by her master with little more than the clothes on her back and forced to leave members of her family behind in captivity. She journeyed to the city, where she eventually came under the protection of El Hor and Messaoud Boulkheir.

Boulkheir introduced me to other escaped slaves, whom he assembled in secret at his home to speak with me. One young woman, M'Barka Mint Bilal, was born in slavery and had run away from her master, leaving her young child and the rest of her family in slavery. Another runaway, Shaba Mint Bilal, also left a family behind. She was later tracked down, jailed, and brought before a judge by her former master. In court, the Arab fabricated a story, telling the judge that she had stolen one of his cattle. When the judge did not release her to him, he claimed that she was his wife and the mother of his two children, who were still living in his home. Still, the judge did not rule in his favor.

Shaba's desire to get her children back was strong. She went to the police for help, but they threatened to put her in chains and return her to slavery if she did not leave the matter alone. Undaunted, Shaba traveled back to her former master's house and confronted him, demanding that he release the children to her. But he told her that her mother and one of the children had died and that he had rented the other child out to another family. None of this was true, of course. The Arab was simply embittered and attempting to hurt her further. He believed, as perhaps all slaveholders do, that this lie, coupled with the severe conditions Shaba would encounter living on her own, would teach her a lesson and force her to submit to his will.

I next spoke to Brahim Ould Maboune, born to a mother and father who were also born slaves. His parents, he told me, were worked very hard by their Beydane master and were frequently severely beaten. As a young man, angered over their situation, he secreted his mother and father away from their master's home and brought them to Nouakchott. His master found him and had him viciously beaten and put in chains. He was left for many weeks in that condition. Upon being released, however, Brahim ran away again, back to Nouakchott. He was determined not to return to slavery. He made a life for himself and his mother in the capital city. When his mother died, the master tracked Brahim down again and demanded all of her earthly goods. Brahim refused and went to SOS-Esclaves and Boubacar Messaoud for legal help. Despite continued threats and harassment from his former master, he tenaciously resisted returning to anything connected with

M'barka Mint Bilal (top). *Brahim Ould Maboune* (bottom)

slave status.

Of all the runaways I spoke with, Aïchanna Mint Abeïd Boïlil's story was the most moving. I met her one evening while I was conducting a long interview with Boubacar Messaoud at his home. His assistant, Leidji Traore, interrupted the interview to announce that Aïchanna had just arrived in Nouakchott after having escaped from slavery via the Mauritanian version of the Underground Railroad. She was being hidden in one of the "safe houses" on that route and wanted to speak with Boubacar. Leidji stated that a case like this one demanded special precautions because some of Aïchanna's relatives, trusted slaves of her master, had been sent to find her and return her to slavery.

The three of us traveled by car to the rendezvous point. We drove for hours, searching to locate the house in the darkness. I soon noticed that everything began looking the same. Apparently, we were lost. We stopped at a number of places, but no luck. After several attempts, we finally located the house, which was hidden behind a small courtyard.

Boubacar got out of the car and went to the door. I watched him intently as he disappeared from sight, expecting him to return at any minute and indicate that we had again approached the wrong house. Instead, he reemerged, smiling and gesturing for us to follow. We had located her at last. To this day I have no idea how he could tell one house from another.

We followed him through the courtyard, passing finally through a narrow doorway into a one-room dwelling with a dirt floor and no electricity. On the floor lay two small children wrapped in blankets. The woman whom we had come to meet, Aïchanna, sat on the floor next to the children, wearing the traditional Arab dress for women. Her head was covered, but her face was not. She was a dark-skinned woman with a very sad expression and a quiet spirit.

We lit a candle. As the light flickered and danced, casting eerie shadows on the rough-hewn walls, Aïchanna told me her story, which Boubacar translated as follows:

My name is Aïchanna Mint Abeïd Boïlil, and I am [a] thirty-year-old descendant of a slave. I have experienced this condition since I was born. I need to make the world aware of the hectic time in which I have been living, which is the separation of my five children [Salma, age fourteen; El Barra, age twelve; Maouloud, age ten; Mohamed Lemine, age six; and Brahim, age four], who have been kept by their master…

The conditions that we lived—myself, my mother, my brothers, and sisters, my father, my cousins, and my children—was very inhuman. We were like animals.

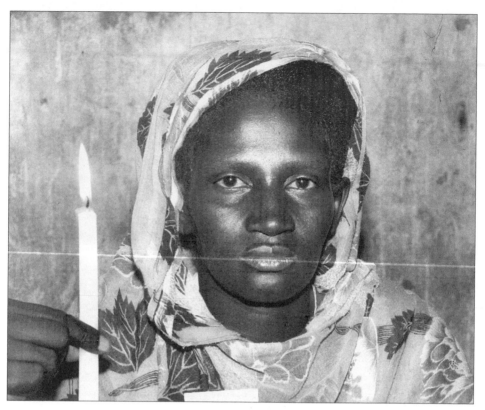

Aïchanna Mint Abeïd Boïlil

We lived in the city of Lemteyin. Our master, Mohamed Ould Moïssa, is well known for his ability to influence and his brutality....He's a farmer and a herder, and he belongs to the tribe of Oulad Bou'liya. Mohamed Ould Moïssa has slaves working for him, and he also rents or lends them to his relatives and friends. My oldest daughter was lent since she was four years old to serve Salka Mint Terrouzi, Mohamed Ould Moïssa's mother-in-law. At the same time, my second daughter was given to the master's daughter, Beida Mint Mohamed Ould Moïssa, when she [Beida] married Youssef Ould Ahmed Chennane, who worked for the administration. My daughter must travel with this family no matter where they go. The last news I have of my daughter's whereabouts is that she is in Aioun, where Youssouf is now working.

My cousin, Nema Mint Ramdane, one of my aunt's daughters, was given purely and simply as **hediya** [a religious gift] to a big **marabout** [religious teacher] of the region, Cheikh Ahmedou

Ould Veten, of the clan of Dachekra and the tribe of Idab Lahssen.
I myself was lent many times to the families of Lemteyin and Nou-
akchott, where I made two visits to the half-brother of my master...

When I understood that slavery is not right, for myself,
I decide to live my freedom, and I came to Nouakchott with my
youngest daughter and my second daughter.

I asked Aïchanna about the father of her children, where and who was he? She explained that her master had paired her with two different men, both slaves, but she no longer knew where they were. I then asked her why her master would not give her children their freedom now that she and they had escaped. Aïchanna looked at Boubacar and then at me with an expression that seemed to indicate that I had asked a silly question. She then quietly replied, "My master will not give me my children because my belly belongs to my master."

I sat there on that dirt floor in the dark, looking intently at this woman and feeling angry at myself for asking a question with such an obvious answer. How could I have forgotten that under Mauritania's unspoken "law," this woman was someone else's legal property? She might just as well have been a chair, or a horse, or a cow. And I had just asked her a question that only drew attention to the life of degradation she had lived since birth!

At that point, I stopped the interview. I was so embarrassed and overwhelmed with guilt, all I wanted to do was get out of that room. I was coming face-to-face with my historical past and a problem that black men have faced with their women since slavery began: that of having to listen to a black woman talk about the troubles she is having with the master and not being able to do a damn thing about it, neither to help or protect her.

Who was I that Aïchanna should have taken such a risk to talk to me? What was I going to do? What resources did I possess that could make a difference in this woman's life? I pushed these thoughts to the back of my mind and turned to Boubacar, who calmly shared more details of Aïchanna's case with me.

Upon arriving in Nouakchott, Boubacar explained, Aïchanna immediately made contact with SOS-Esclaves, which arranged for her hiding place and began fighting with the government to reunite her with her other children. Though her case was especially problematic, it was also especially useful to the Haratine freedom fighters' movement because Aïchanna claimed to know the names of each of the Arab families who held her children in slavery. She also stated that she could cite the names and ages of the twenty-four slaves currently owned by her master. Messaoud explained to me that this is valuable information for Mauritania's anti-slavery organizations, which are trying to gather as much information as possible that documents the existence of slavery. They need this information in order to make a case, for individual Africans as well as generally, to the Mauritanian government to uphold its "official" emancipation laws.

After she finished relating the details of her situation through my comrade's interpretation, Aïchanna turned to me and looked deeply into my eyes. Her stare felt as if it was burning an impression onto the back of my skull, as if she was shining a light on my mind, trying to read my thoughts in an area where language could not suffice. Sputtering but sincerely, I thanked her for talking to me and asked Boubacar to tell her that there were many people in the United States who were working to stop the practice of slavery and help her get her children back.

I reached out and took her hand in both of my hands. I held it for a long time—I don't know exactly how long—and we just stood there, staring at each other.

I was thinking: Here I am, holding the hand of a black slave woman who is hiding from her master. I am holding hands with my history, the history of my people, whom I had long felt in my heart but had never been in real contact with before.

As I stood there, I reflected on the incredible suffering that this proud, soft-spoken woman had experienced throughout her life, and I suddenly felt very sad and helpless. I knew that there was nothing I could do for her right then, and I wondered if I could ever do anything for her in the future. But to myself, I promised to do all that I could to help her and others break free from the mental, physical, and psychological shackles of slavery. I promised.

I squeezed Aïchanna's hand one last time, hugged her, and walked back to the car. As we rode back in silence, I remember feeling numb and disconnected from everything. I kept hearing a voice in my head saying, "What the hell is this, man? What has happened to our people?"

◈　　◈　　◈

I had many more such experiences and conversations every day I spent in Mauritania. From them, one of the most painful lessons I learned was that women and children are the most vulnerable groups insofar as the institution of slavery is concerned. They are its principal victims, regardless of whether one is referring to antebellum America or twentieth century northwestern Africa.

I learned that the body of the female slave in the Mauritanian context is seen first and foremost as a vehicle for reproduction. The slave woman's children belong to the master, whether he has fathered them or not. Slave fathers have no rights over their own offspring. Thus, because technically they have no dependents, it is relatively easy for male slaves to run away, leaving their children and slave women to fend for themselves after they flee to the cities, where they usually end up languishing or working in menial jobs.

The situation is much more difficult for the women left behind. The female slave's every move is decided by her master, who expects and often takes sexual liberties with her as a matter of course. If he so chooses, the master, not the woman's own family, gives her away in marriage, and any marriage he does not approve is considered void. Slave women are frequently beaten and humiliated in public and privately for the most insignificant infractions.

The master is also free to do what he likes with the children of his slaves. Like their mothers, slave children are used for various domestic, craft, or agricultural tasks. This includes minding the herds of their masters as well as those of other families in the master's clan. Slave children can also be given or sold to other families or individuals at the whims of their masters. Some have even been sent to the Gulf states, where they are in demand as camel jockeys. True to form, the Mauritanian government has shown no concern for the welfare of the black African children held in bondage in its midst. Child labor is considered the norm in Mauritania, and young people, even very young people, are exploited in the work place regardless of status. Especially so those who are slaves.

It is difficult for slave mothers to escape from their masters with their children and, as a result, most are reluctant to do so. When the women do decide to run away because their circumstances become unbearable, they frequently must leave their children behind and can only regain custody of them with great difficulty. Alone or with their children, runaway slave women have to cope with many difficulties. In the cities, it is extremely hard for them to find a way to live decently and independent of their masters. This leaves these women with few options. They can either work as servants for middle-income families, become merchants in the marketplaces, do manual labor, or become prostitutes. Because their children have never been issued birth certificates, they cannot go to school and usually end up running the streets.

❧ ❧ ❧

The case of Zgheilina, another of the Haratine runaways, is illustrative of the plight of African women in slavery. As a child in the 1940s, Zgheilina lived in Selibaby in the southernmost region of the country. She was kidnapped when she was twelve years old by two members of the northern Mauritanian Rgueibat tribe. They rebaptized her Fatma Mint Matalla in an attempt to make her forget her origins. For thirty years, she was their slave until, in 1992, following the injury of her master's son by a grenade, she had the opportunity to accompany the wounded boy to the city of Zouerate. There, she met a Haratine anti-slavery activist who listened to her tragedy and helped her to escape and return to Selibaby.

M'Barka Mint Said's case was a similar tale of victimization and woe minus the victory of freedom. As Boubacar Messaoud explained to me, when M'Barka was in her teens, her mother, Dadou Mint Madembe, was asked by the former husband of her mistress to "lend" him her daughter for a two-month period. Having really little choice in the matter, Dadou agreed, only to find out some time later that this man sold M'Barka to another Arab, an official of the Saudi Arabian-owned Petromin Oil Company, who had taken her out of the country. The mother went to the police to complain but was told that there was nothing they could do. Years later, M'Barka got the opportunity to return to Mauritania with her new master. Although her mother continued to fight for her return, M'Barka's master never agreed to give her her freedom.

◈　◈　◈

I was amazed at the number of cases confirming the reality of slavery that Boubacar Messaoud and Messaoud Boulkheir were able to present to me. Their organizations were compiling the evidence presented by black Africans such as Shaba Mint Bilal, M'Barka Mint Bilal, Jebada Maouloud, Brahim Ould Maboune, Aïchanna Mint Abeid Boilil, Zgheilina, and M'Barka Mint Said to confront the Mauritanian government on this issue. But that government, for its part, continued to deny the truth, for the truth would reveal Arab complicity in a crime of heinous proportions. It would destroy a carefully knit curtain of shame.

◈　◈　◈

One evening, Boubacar Messaoud and I were talking about the United States, its role in and responses to the issue of slavery in Mauritania. Had anyone ever presented these cases to the U.S. ambassador? I asked him. The person in that position at that time was Dorothy Sampas. I mentioned a *Washington Times* article I had read prior to my visit in which Sampas stated that she had never been given any concrete evidence on the existence of present-day slavery in Mauritania.

Boubacar smiled, but I could see anger and frustration in his eyes. He rifled through his briefcase and pulled out a batch of folders, which he placed before me. Then he leaned forward and said, "Sam, you know for yourself that it is a lie! Madame Sampas has been informed. I *know* that she has! I have spoken with her myself on this issue. She may not know about all of the cases, but she knows about many of them. She and everyone else in the country knows quite a bit about this problem because we in the anti-slavery movement have placed articles and information about many cases in the Mauritanian newspaper *Le Calame*."

Continuing, his otherwise affable countenance changed and his smile turned into a grimace. For her role in supporting the Beydane regime, Boubacar claimed that Madame Sampas was widely disliked and distrusted by Mauritania's Negro-Africans and Haratines. She was so closely aligned with the racist, murderous policies of the Mauritanian government, he said, that communicating with her constituted a risk to the anti-slavery movement.

"Madame Sampas," he stated, "is not very honest on this question, and she believes all of the lies that the Mauritanian government has told her! You know, the government tries to project the idea that all that is left is the vestiges of slavery. It creates these pseudo-organizations, such as those whose purpose is to appear to feed the former slaves. But they are simply fronts—empty shells—to give outsiders the impression that slavery is a problem of the past. Madame Sampas and so many others, when they come to Mauritania, they just look at the 'official story.' They are such fools!"

"Brother Sam, we hope you will look at all of the cases we have presented you and inform others in the United States that slavery is a massive problem in Mauritania, especially in the countryside. There is still a huge trafficking in slaves going on between Mauritania and the Arab Emirate States."

"I know I have shown and told you about a lot," Boubacar said, reaching back into his briefcase and pulling out a file containing a tattered newspaper article. "But let me share with you just one more case."

I began reading the article he had handed me and saw that it was published in *Le Calame* on August 9, 1995. It was about a young girl named Fatimetou Mint Rabi Ould Ely of the village of N'Doumely. Fatimetou was the fourteen-year-old daughter of a former slave woman who had escaped from slavery and died in 1980. She lived with her uncle for five years afterward until one day the authorities suddenly came into her village and forcibly took her away.

"That's right!" Boubacar exclaimed, interrupting my reading as if he knew exactly the point in the text that I had reached. "The governor of Guidimagha, Yahya Ould Sidi Moustaph himself, gave the order to do so! He sent his assistant, Mohamed Ould El Gouth, who is in charge of Economic Affairs, along with a military escort, and they just carried her off! Just like that, with no explanation!"

I continued reading. After fighting through a lot of government red tape, the article maintained that the uncle learned that Fatimetou had been sold to an Arab named Abdel Wehab Ould Ahmed Jiddou, who had bought the girl from one of his uncles, who at one time had owned Fatimetou's mother prior to her escape. Abdel Jiddou and his family were asserting, the government maintained, their enduring rights to inherit the offspring of their property.

Because slavery was supposed to have been officially abolished, Fatimetou's family pressed charges to get her back. In court, the Arabs refused to reveal Fatimetou's whereabouts. To this day, Boubacar told me, she has not been found. His arms dropping to his side, he said remorsefully that one can only assume that Fatimetou has disappeared into the abyss of slavery.

❖ ❖ ❖

Boubacar looked at his watch and politely indicated that he had to cut our interview short to go to a meeting. As I rose to thank him, he was already on his feet, preparing to leave. I stood there for a minute, watching as he busily collected reams of files and papers and stuffed them into his already bulging briefcase. I was in awe of his energy and dedication, his amazing ability to work around the clock, tirelessly, for this noble cause.

As I waited for a ride back to my hosts' home, I reflected on my trip and what I had achieved thus far. My visit had been successful. My research had progressed beyond every goal I had hoped for. I had the pictures, the videotape, and the sound recordings conclusively documenting the existence of slavery in Mauritania and Senegal. The evidence was overwhelming.

Still, there was so much more that I wanted to do, so much more evidence that I wanted to collect. I wanted to arrange an interview with Abdel Nasser Sid Ahmed Yessa, a Mauritanian Arab whom I had heard was very active in the anti-slavery movement, to ascertain his role in and views on the struggle. But all of my contacts in Nouakchott were telling me that it was time to go. Even Hapsa Dia had said that I should lay low and get a flight out of the country as soon as possible. Upon recapture or under pressure from the authorities, she warned, one of the several runaways I had interviewed might inform the government about my investigation.

Mr. B. reminded me that my newfound knowledge had placed upon me a great responsibility. He wanted it to reach the United States quickly and safely so that the American people could learn for themselves about the suffering that is going on in his country. He said this, even though he and the others knew that the release of my findings in the United States might cause an uproar in Mauritania and put in jeopardy the lives of all those who had helped me gather my information. Still, he said, it was their responsibility to put their lives and freedom on the line to make sure that one day everyone in Mauritania would be free.

◈　　◈　　◈

That night, even as I struggled with my feelings of guilt about the potential danger my friends might face, I took precautions to ensure that all of my videotapes and audiotapes were carefully packed for the trip back to Senegal. I spent the next few days checking and rechecking my notes and trying to clear up anything that I did not understand. I had Hapsa Dia go over the important documents she had translated into English for me and rework any points that were still unclear until they were understandable. My hosts made sure that all of the arrangements for my departure were in order.

I became increasingly anxious to get out of Mauritania and back to Senegal where I could begin organizing all of my data. The evening my flight was to leave finally came. My hosts drove me to the airport. I got through customs without incident. We all hugged each other, fighting back tears.

Here I was, I thought, getting on a plane, going back to America to try and raise hell over this issue, yet I was flying out of danger into freedom and they were staying in the middle of the battlefield. Notwithstanding, the expressions on their faces said: We are unafraid. The image of my friends, standing there on the ground waving to me as I climbed the stairs to the airplane, was burned into my memory forever.

As my plane lifted off, I thought about seeing my friend and brother Mamadou Bocar Ba again. I leaned back in my seat. I had done what I had come to Africa for.

RETURN TO SENEGAL

The jet landed safely in Dakar, bringing me from the living past to the present. As at the beginning of my journey, Mamadou was there, waiting for me.

We hugged each other, and after standing back and looking at me, he laughed and said, "You have been to Mauritania, Samuel Cotton! What do you think of that crazy place? Was the trip successful?"

I told him it most certainly was and started to tell him about everything that had transpired. We laughed and talked as we picked up my suitcases full of precious cargo, exited customs, and left the terminal. The night was warm and full of the sounds of a bustling city. There they were, the army of cab drivers, the markets, and the crowds of people. Life, freedom, vitality,

Nassar Sid Ahmed Yessa

and energy was in the night air. I was home. I felt safe again.

Mamadou hailed a taxi and, as is the tradition, started to bargain with the driver over the fare. He turned to me and shook his head, "He's crazy! He wants too much!" He hailed another taxi and haggled with the cabbie until he was satisfied. We got in and were on our way. I wondered if the waterbugs and ticks had missed me. As it turned out, it wasn't going to matter.

◈   ◈   ◈

As we approached Ouagou Niayes Two, Mamadou asked if I was hungry and told me that our hosts had prepared another big dinner for me. I told him I was famished. As the taxi pulled up in front of the house, all of its occupants rushed out to greet me. Omar and Bocar Ba and many others were there. The kissing and hugging were so profuse, it was like a hero's homecoming. I was humbled and overjoyed.

Soon everyone was back inside and in the back of the house, busily attending to the preparations for the sumptuous meal Mamadou had promised. For a few moments, I was alone by myself in the big room where all would soon gather to eat and talk, waiting for Mamadou to return with a bowl of chicken, potatoes, vegetables, and a bottle of my favorite soda, orange Fanta.

Suddenly, in the quiet, a vision of Hapsa Dia's face—the way that she looked at me at the airport—came flooding back into my mind. As if she were in the room beside me, I heard her voice: "Are you going to do anything with all the things we risked to provide you with? Are you going to go home and forget us?"

I was immediately filled with an overpowering sense of sadness and guilt. All of the adrenaline that had carried me through the trip back to Senegal and into Dakar, all of the energy that had counterbalanced the constant stress I had been working under, was instantly drained out of me. I sank back heavily into the chair I was sitting in.

Thoughts of Aïchanna Boilil and her two children sleeping on the dirt floor of their darkened room rushed over me. Thoughts of Fatimetou being dragged from her uncle's home by the police overtook me. The images of Shaba Bilal's rotted and swollen hands and of Brahim Maboune languishing for days in chains for refusing to tell his master the whereabouts of his escaped parents swept in and around in my mind like hundreds of fluttering sparrows.

I broke down and wept again. I was like a burst balloon, and all the air was rushing out of me. Suddenly I had neither energy nor appetite. Mamadou came into the room with my bowl of food and asked what was wrong. I simply told him that I did not feel well and just wanted to go and lay down.

❖ ❖ ❖

I stayed in that state for two days. For two days, I lay in my room sleeping, and when awake, staring at the ceiling. If the ticks and waterbugs were there, I don't remember them or recall even having been concerned about them.

Mamadou would frequently come to the wire-meshed window and ask if I was alright, if I was going to eat something. All I would tell him was, "Mamadou, I just need to rest."

On the third day, my strength and spirit returned. I was in a positive mood. I rose and ate a breakfast of hard-boiled eggs, buttered bread, and coffee. I remember that breakfast vividly because I was so very hungry. After breakfast, I began checking and reorganizing all of my data materials for the trip back to the States.

◈　　◈　　◈

In January 18, 1996, thanks to the protection of my ancestors, my flight from Dakar successfully navigated its way through dangerous fog to land at Kennedy International Airport. But returning to the United States was only the beginning of another arduous journey. On March 13, I was to testify before the House Subcommittee on International Operations and Human Rights about slavery in Mauritania.

CHAPTER SEVEN

~~~~~~

*W*ith regard to Mauritania, the State Department's Human
Rights Report seems to have changed dramatically from last
year....This year's report says nothing whatsoever about those
slaves, as if they simply disappeared. Similarly, the report of the State Department states that, "Tens of thousands of persons whose ancestors were
slaves still occupy positions of servitude."

I do not understand the State Department's distinction between being
a slave and occupying a position of servitude, and we hope that the distinction becomes clear today. To say, as this year's Human Rights Report
does, that these people remain in servitude because of their lack of knowledge about their own status is to confirm that they are still slaves and are
treated as slaves by their masters. This is an important issue and one that
deserves and indeed demands Congressional action.[1]

—ILEANA ROS-LEHTINEN, Chair, House Subcommittee
on Africa, Committee on International Relations)

THE HEARING

It was March 13, 1996, a sunny but cold day, when I arrived in Washington, D.C., to testify before Congress on the question of contemporary
slavery in northwestern Africa. The Subcommittee hearings were in large
part the result of the tireless activities of Barbara Ledeen of the Independent
Women's Forum. An outstanding advocate for human rights and for the
rights of women, Barbara had worked hard to bring this issue to the attention of official Washington, and her work was bearing fruit today.

Barbara had also arranged for me to speak at a press conference for the

National Abolitionist Council, which is the umbrella organization for all of the abolitionist groups operating in the United States. The briefing was to be held that morning at Howard University's new Ralph J. Bunche International Center, and I was looking forward to addressing an audience of black college students and informing them about the silent terror—the ongoing nightmare of degradation their African kinfolk were plagued with even now, in this, the twentieth century.

However, my experience warned me that very few African-American students would show up, much less show any interest in the issue. I had hoped that Howard University would take a stand and offer a statement condemning the Mauritanian and Sudanese governments, but I wasn't optimistic about that, either. I would be right on both assumptions.

Fewer than twelve Howard students showed up for the press conference. Julius Coles, the Bunche Center's director, set the tone before the program began by stating that "there are many points of view" on the slavery issue and stressing that "Howard University takes no position on it."

Upon hearing this, a smile crossed the face of the Mauritanian Ambassador, Bilal Ould Werzeg, who was seated in the front row, directly across from the speakers' table. He had come with three of his aides. Also in attendance were two officials from the Sudanese embassy, who were quietly taping the proceedings. While these representatives offered no formal rebuttal, they did distribute a printed statement, which charged that my research and the afternoon's planned hearings were propaganda "organized by certain circles hostile to the Sudan and its orientation."

Still, I thought the press conference went off pretty well. Although the room was not filled with the people I had hoped to see, the media coverage was excellent. Most importantly, reporters and cameramen from "Dateline NBC" were there. Before the year was over, that program would produce an excellent documentary on slavery in Sudan, marking the first time that the issue would be addressed by a major television network.

As I left the press conference with my comrades from various organizations in the anti-slavery movement, my mind was racing ahead, toward the afternoon's events.

◈   ◈   ◈

At two-thirty, I was to testify before Congress. My principal "opponent" would be the U.S. State Department, represented by Deputy Assistant Secretary of the Bureau of African Affairs William H. Twaddell. Twaddell had been sent to bolster the State Department's current position that modern slavery did not exist in Mauritania. Under his watch, the State Department had done an about-face on its earlier reports confirming the existence of massive slavery there.

For its part, the Mauritanian government was trotting out its big guns to square off against me and my research findings. It had hired a Washington insider whose job it would be to counter all of the assertions I planned to make before the Subcommittee. That man would be an African-American, a former member of Congress and former chairman of the House Subcommittee on Africa, who was presently serving as a "legislative advocate" for the Islamic Republic of Mauritania. His name was Mervyn Dymally, and he had been specifically commissioned by the Mauritanian government on this day to deny the existence of slavery in that nation and among its allies.

The Subcommittee hearings were to be held in the Rayburn House Office Building on Capitol Hill. After a quick lunch, we rushed across town to the Rayburn building and made our way through the wide corridors to Room 2172.

It was two-fifteen. The large, stately chamber was buzzing with activity. The back of the room was lined with television cameras and packed with spectators and reporters. As I took my seat at the table where I was to deliver my testimony, I was warmly greeted by many of my Mauritanian and Sudanese comrades in the anti-slavery movement. I noticed immediately that Barbara Ledeen had enlarged several of the photographs I had taken of slaves I interviewed in Mauritania, and she had strategically placed them right in front of the galley where the Congressional committee members were seated. The effect was powerful. The sad eyes of the disenfranchised would be in the direct line of sight of all those who would be presenting testimony this day.

The hearings were quickly called to order and the proceedings began. I was asked to deliver my statement, the gist of which follows:

Thank you, Mr. Chairman and members of the Subcommittee. I am Samuel Cotton, a Ph.D. candidate in social policy at Columbia University and the executive director of the Coalition Against Slavery in Mauritania and Sudan. Between December 23, 1995, and January 17, 1996, I conducted ethnographic research in Senegal and Mauritania on the practice of slavery, utilizing camera, audio-, and video-recording devices. There, I recorded interviews with black Mauritanians in the refugee camps of N'dioum, Boki-Diawe, Wourossogui, and Horkadiere, who provided testimony which supported the charge that slavery is still a way of life in Mauritania and has simply shifted from an overt to a covert practice. I also interviewed Mauritanian refugees in Dakar, Senegal, as I was interested in examining and finding out if the work of Mau-

ritanian historian Garba Diallo, in which he describes the common practice of transporting slaves from Mauritania across the Senegal River into Senegal, was valid. I have documents to prove that such traffic exists.

I arrived in Mauritania on January 2, 1996, and departed January 12, 1996. I conducted interviews with the leaders of two anti-slavery organizations: Messaoud Ould Boulkheir, president of El Hor; and Boubacar Messaoud, president of SOS-Esclaves. Both leaders informed me that African slaves are kept in bondage by a combination of physical restraint, psychological domination, religious manipulation, and the lack of government interest in creating programs that would enable slaves to make the transition to freedom. Boubacar Messaoud noted that slavery is massive in Mauritania, especially in the countryside, and he maintained that there is also trafficking in slaves between Mauritania and the Arab Emirate States.

...From my interviews with Haratines, or freed slaves, and with runaway slaves, I learned that the government of Mauritania does not penalize slaveowners, nor has it created any concrete programs to end the practice of slavery....And because there are no concrete programs or any anti-slavery laws with teeth in them, the Arab populations of Mauritania and other parts of northwestern Africa carry on the business of slavery as they have for centuries.

Open slave markets are clearly a thing of the past. The difference is that today the buying and selling of slaves takes place in the houses of Moors and via private arrangements between Arab families. Slave marriages continue to be arranged such that strong black males are placed with strong black females, and the Arab families who arrange these "marriages" divide up their rights to the children born of these unions. Slave women are bred many times by different slave men and their children become the property of the master. For example, when I asked the escaped slavewoman Aïchanna Mint Abeid Boilil why her master continued to hold her children in bondage, she stated, "Because my belly belongs to my master." Her testimony, and that of four other runaway slaves and one freed slave—one male and four females—was recorded.

It is important to me that the U.S. State Department listen to the people in bondage and not to the oppressive government of Mauritania. The shift in the language of the State Department from stating that slavery exists to stating that slavery is over and that only the vestiges of slavery remain in Mauritania is disturbing.

If slavery is over in Mauritania, when did this great event occur? Who observed the freeing of over ninety thousand people? How and with what methods were the slaves informed that they were physically and spiritually free? Where are the interviews which indicate, as the Mauritanian government contends, that freed slaves choose to remain in bondage simply for economic reasons? What record is there of provisions being made for their physical needs such as food, clothing, and shelter? How were they protected from their masters to keep the latter from recapturing them and returning them to slavery?

What governmental or international organization monitored and evaluated the success of what would have had to have been a stupendous undertaking? Why didn't the Mauritanian government allow the political parties of the free or Negro-Africans and the anti-slavery organizations of the freed slaves to monitor this major event since slavery is at the top of these groups' agendas?

There are no valid answers to these questions because no empirical data nor any studies conducted by experienced investigators such as the London-based Anti-Slavery Society exists to support the statements of the State Department or those of the U.S. Ambassador to Mauritania, Ms. Dorothy Sampas....Does the State Department really believe that a system of slavery that began before the American slave trade and that has continued to this very day will not require concrete and measurable interventions to stop it?

I continued, noting the plight of Mauritanian refugees who had been ethnically cleansed from their homelands in 1989. I cited the outrage of Amadou Boubou Niang, the president of the Association of Mauritanian Refugees in Senegal, over Ambassador Sampas's statement that his people preferred refugee status because it enabled them to receive free food and a chance to go to the United States. As I expressed to the Subcommittee:

These people [Mauritanian refugees]...go down to the river and stare across the river at their farms, at the people who own their cattle now. They had villages. They were businessmen and businesswomen. They were prosperous people. They were hardworking. Their centers of commerce were in the south. How is it that suddenly they have acquired great and massive character defects, and have become lazy and want to live off crumbs?

Lastly, I implicated and castigated Ambassador Sampas for the role she played in support of the Mauritanian government and Arab slaveholders:

I recorded an interview that I conducted with members of The Widows, an organization of Negro-African Mauritanian women whose husbands, sons, and brothers were tortured to death and murdered. They constantly go to speak to the U.S. Ambassador, who tells them to forget about the issue. "Life is like that," Sampas was noted as telling this group during an interview. "Don't push things," she said. So there is a strong feeling among the people, ex-slave and free, that the United States is in harmony with slavery and oppression because Ambassador Sampas espouses and supports whatever the government says.

The Honorable Christopher Smith of New Jersey, chairman of the Subcommittee, was quick to speak up after I concluded my remarks. "Mr. Cotton," Smith rumbled, "thank you for those comments. I'd like to note hat one of the biggest concerns we have on this Subcommittee is that of the whitewashing and belittling of crimes against humanity, and certainly slavery fits that definition. Last year, we had a hearing, a series of hearings actually, on the State Department's country reports on human rights practices, and one of the more telling comments by representatives of Amnesty International was that this Administration treated human rights as if it were on an island, with no connection to policy...which suggests that raising human rights issues is simply an exercise in exposing a crime and then doing nothing."

"In the case of Mauritania," he continued, "this apparent rewriting of reality—and we are going to delve much further into this—raises the specter of the U.S. government misinforming and becoming part of the whitewashing of these atrocities."

◈   ◈   ◈

It was now time for my adversaries to take their turn at bat, to make their statements and be questioned by the Subcommittee members. It was time for an historical drama as old as slavery itself to play itself out on the floor of Congress.

The first to speak was Mervyn Dymally. He began by briefly identifying himself and went hurriedly into his statement, as follows:

Mr. Chairman and members of the Subcommittee, the Mauritanian government is pleased to have this opportunity to address the question of the existence of vestiges of slavery in the Republic of Mauritania. Let me say at the outset that no one in Mauritania denies the fact that at one time slavery existed there. Yet, since its independence, Mauritania has moved toward the abolishment of chattel slavery as it was known prior to independence.

On several occasions, there have been issued presidential orders and amendments to the Mauritanian constitution addressing this subject. The current government has made it abundantly clear that slavery will not be tolerated in Mauritania.

...To show their commitment to the abolishment of slavery, the Mauritanians have sent, since 1993, three delegations to the United States, two of which I was intimately involved with. I took one of these delegations headed by the president of the Mauritanian senate, who in American terms would be considered black, to Arizona to meet with Reverend Leon Sullivan and the leadership of the African-American Summit.

At this point, Dymally was interrupted by Congressman Smith. "Mr. Dymally," Smith broke in, "China does the same thing. Cuba does it as well, as the gentlelady and chair of the Subcommittee on Africa, Ms. Ileana Ros-Lehtinen, has pointed out. They can show you chapter and verse on paper, but the reality in these nations is far from the stated beliefs, or at least the articulated beliefs, expressed in their official documents."

It was obvious from his comments that Congressman Smith was going to be critical of the Mauritanian government's star witness. He next asked the former Congressman to shed some light on a very important point before the hearings proceeded further.

"Mr. Dymally," he asked, "you are a paid lobbyist for the government of Mauritania, are you not?" Dymally nodded and answered, "Yes." "For the record, then," Smith continued, "could you state what your salary is? It would be helpful to our deliberations."

Dymally replied, candidly but somewhat ruffled, "One hundred-twenty thousand dollars."

It was like old times in African history, and all the old players were present. Here was a man of African descent, a man whose ancestors had been slaves, a prominent statesman, and former chairman of the House Subcommittee on Africa, who was flagrantly identifying himself as an advocate for a government that supported a system that, were he but on Mauritanian soil, would smile upon his purchase, and that of many of his relatives, for the price he had just quoted as his salary for representing it.

From an historical perspective, Dymally was functioning in these hearings in the same capacity that the African middleman functioned during the trans-Atlantic and sub-Saharan slave trade. He was a paid instrument of Arab slavers, and for the right price, he was selling both slave and free Africans in Mauritania down the proverbial river.

Mervyn Dymally was an important part of the Mauritanian government's time-tested strategy of putting token black faces up front as "proof" that slavery doesn't exist in Mauritania and that it is really a land of equal opportunity. He was being used before the U.S. Congress in much the same way that Bilal Ould Werzeg, the Mauritanian Ambassador to the United States, was being used. When the Mauritanian government began to feel pressure from the abolitionist movement, Werzeg, a Haratine, had been appointed to this position to ameliorate the opposition and paint a pretty face on Mauritania's treachery.

In similar fashion, without doing any research of their own to find out the truth, Dymally, Werzeg, and U.S. Ambassador Sampas were, in effect, serving as mouthpieces for the Mauritanian government. Whenever Congress, other Africans, or anyone else raised the issue of slavery and human rights abuses in Mauritania, these three would march up to the presidential palace and respectfully ask President Maaouya Ould Sid Ahmed Taya if the allegations were true. Of course, they would more than likely discuss them over a lavishly prepared state dinner or lunch and there would probably be, as Dymally's extravagant salary alluded, plenty of envelopes passing under the table. But if President Taya replied that slavery did not exist, then that was the view they would espouse.

◈　　◈　　◈

Not wanting to appear a middleman and in an effort to protect both his own image and that of his employers, Dymally entreated, "Can I go on, Mr. Chairman? I did not know that I was on trial here....I am simply here to express a point of view, not to criticize anybody's testimony or to deny it. I want to let you know that this is a matter which I take up at least twice a year when I go to Mauritania, and I have frequently communicated to Mauritanian officials American Congressional unhappiness over this subject."

To this, Smith responded, "You know, Mr. Dymally, you said you were not on trial, but you are a spokesman representing the Mauritanian government. I do not think it is fair to say that you are acting in a neutral position or just as a conduit of information back and forth, which is why I asked about your sources of information. Do you agree with the State Department's assessment that slavery has virtually disappeared in Mauritania?"

"Yes," Dymally replied.

"You do?" asked Smith. "Have you heard anything here today that would cast some doubt on that?"

Again Dymally replied "yes," referring to my earlier testimony. But by his position, Dymally had shown that he knew nor cared nothing about the blacks in Mauritania. His business was making money, and he had no problem representing a racist government as long as he received his pieces of silver. Yet under the deluge of testimony I presented from my interviews, my mountains of videotaped and audiotaped evidence, even Dymally had to admit that he had learned several things at these hearings that he had not known before.

◈　◈　◈

State Department representative William Twaddell was the next to address the panel, which had earlier begun scrutinizing the astonishing about-face taken by the State Department in its 1995 country report on human rights practices in Mauritania. I too had read that report and concluded that it made no historical or contemporary sense. In it, the State Department adopted the Mauritanian government's "party line"—hook, line, and sinker—and played it like a broken record.

The document repeatedly dodges the "s" word, referring to "vestiges" and the "legacy" of slavery, and using the words like "servitude" and "near servitude" to describe the black Mauritanian reality. It also backs off from accepting as accurate the number of slaves (ninety thousand) that the London-based Anti-Slavery Society estimated were living in bondage in Mauritania in 1981. Ironically, Twaddell chose to read to the panel the following excerpt from that very report, which capsulizes some of the State Department's most outrageous and duplicitous claims (emphasis mine):

> *Mauritania has officially abolished slavery several times, most recently in 1980. Nevertheless, the **legacy** of slavery remains in its economic and psychological manifestations. And there are reports of persons continuing to live in conditions of **involuntary servitude. Tens of thousands of persons whose ancestors were slaves still occupy positions of servitude and near servitude,** although such practices as coercive slavery and commerce in slaves appear to have virtually disappeared. In most cases, those remaining in a situation of unpaid or poorly paid servitude do so for lack of better alternatives or **lack of knowledge about their own status.** Some freed slaves, Haratines, have either stayed with or returned to their former masters and continue to provide labor in exchange for room, board and other basic necessities. Others live independently but continue in a symbiotic relationship with their former masters, performing occasional paid or unpaid labor in exchange for food, clothing and medical care.*

> *There are no **reliable statistics for the number of Haratines** who continue to work for the same families for which they worked before the emancipation of 1980, whether as paid or unpaid labor. Reports of cases of involuntary servitude are rare and unconfirmed.*[2]

Suspicious of this line of reasoning, Congressman Victor O. Frazier, an Independent from the U.S. Virgin Islands, immediately bore in with a strong line of questioning.

"Mr. Twaddell," he began, "when you testified that slavery has either been abolished or that only vestiges of slavery exist, could you tell us how and when the blacks were emancipated?" Frazier did not stop there. Before Twaddell could answer the first question, he was peeling off several others, questions that were very similar to those I had raised in my own testimony. "Was there some public pronouncement in the international press?" Frazier queried, "Were there international observers? Where did the former slaves go? And how were their former masters compensated?"

Twaddell replied by citing the three dates that slavery had been abolished in Mauritania, detailing the July 5, 1980, proclamation of manumission by President Haidallah in particular. He also claimed that the Mauritanian government had issued radio announcements informing the slaves that they were free.

My comrades and I laughed to ourselves at his ignorance. What slave, we were thinking, would be sitting by a radio in the middle of the desert, listening to the news?

Twaddell's canned responses were apparently rattling Frazier, who asked, "Mr. Twaddell, segregation was ended in the United States many years ago by proclamation, but there are still vestiges of it. Are you prepared to claim, as a representative of the State Department, that slavery no longer exists in Mauritania—that there is no one being held in slavery in that country—simply because some high-sounding proclamations were issued?"

Twaddell went back on the defensive. "I am prepared to cite, Mr. Congressman, as I did a few minutes ago, the language of our human rights report, which was issued to the Congress last week, in which we talk about the continuation of instances, in the tens of thousands, of servitude and near servitude." He paused for a moment to examine some papers on the table before him, then he gave himself a back door to escape out of by stating, "However, let me make the additional point that we have not seen *evidence* of the buying and selling of human beings or of the *practice* of chattel slavery in Mauritania in 1995 or in recent years."

Frazier wasn't going to let him off the hook that easily. "But are you not, in fact, double-speaking to me if you say that there are 'vestiges' of slavery, while also claiming that you have not seen any evidence of the exchange of people for money or evidence of people being treated, as we are calling them here, as chattel? The question I have to ask is whether the State Department is claiming that slavery does not exist in Mauritania?"

"When I say 'vestiges of slavery,' Congressman," Twaddell responded,

"I am talking about servitude and semi-servitude. I do not think that is slavery itself. It think that is a *vestige* of slavery."

Frazier was clearly perturbed. "Are we playing with words here? Is this not just a fancy way of saying that the State Department will not say there is no slavery in Mauritania but it *will* say that perhaps there are people who work and do not get paid against their will?"

Twaddell refused to concede, even though he didn't have a leg to stand on. "I think that there are people who work and do not get paid. I think there are people who work for well under the Mauritanian government's indicated minimum wage. I call that servitude. I do not call that buying and selling human beings."

How, I wondered, as I sat there in the austere chambers of the House office building, in the belly of the government of the most powerful nation in the world, could an intelligent man like Twaddell confuse vestiges with the actual state of slavery? I had been to Mauritania and had found and documented the cases, person by person, place by place, and time by time. I could go back there right now and pick up folder after folder detailing the very thing that Twaddell was saying he had no knowledge of.

Frazier persisted. "And based on the time you spent there, Mr. Twaddell, can you say today that slavery does not exist in Mauritania? Forget about all you have read and what you have told me has been written." He stressed each word for emphasis, "Does...slavery...exist...in...Mauritania?"

"I would feel very uncomfortable saying, as a certainty, that slavery does not exist," Twaddell replied hesitantly, choosing his words carefully. "Mauritania is a vast country. There are parts of it that, until the droughts of the mid-seventies and eighties, were totally out of the reach of the capital."

It was then that Twaddell broke from the standard script. "I think," he stated next, "it is very conceivable that the practice of slavery continues in very remote parts of that vast desert country."

With that, Congressman David Funderburk of North Carolina jumped into the foray and fired a broadside of his own.

"Mr. Secretary," he asked tersely, "regarding your comment on underground slavery in Mauritania, is it not a severe indictment of the U.S. State Department and foreign service when officers can be working for years in a place and not come up with credible first-hand evidence or documentation of the evils going on all around them? I witnessed this type of blindness to reality when a dictator in Bucharest was killing people and destroying a society. And it was all conveniently overlooked."

"If the United States was really interested and really tried," he continued, "do you not think it could get the evidence or would already have had the evidence it needed?"

Twaddell shuffled some more papers on the table in front of him. "I repeat that we would be delighted to have a good lead, Mr. Congressman, and we would pursue it with whomever..."

Funderburk interrupted him. "What are the foreign service officers *doing* there, then?" he asked.

Twaddell replied, "They are reporting on the situation that they find on the ground, sir."

"They must be blind!" the Congressman from North Carolina concluded, understandably irate and embarrassed by the State Department's lack of candor.

It was clear to me at this point that the Congressional investigators were aware that, at the very least, someone in the State Department was guilty of gross incompetence, and at the worst, of a political cover-up. Once again, powerful others were realizing that Africans were being sacrificed for political gains. They were seeing and hearing for themselves that the United States had evidenced no concern for the misery of those who were being enslaved and disenfranchised in their native land. It had only been concerned about the wooing of a dubious ally.

◈　◈　◈

As Congressman Smith made his concluding remarks, I shuddered as I reflected on Twaddell's and Dymally's testimonies. What if I had not gone to Africa and become a dissenting voice? I wondered. What if there had been no one to refute these two "respected" figures, whose heads, hearts, eyes, and ears were obviously buried in the sand insofar as slavery and oppression in Africa were concerned?

The results would have been tragic. Twaddell's and Dymally's testimony would have been the last word. They would have presented an inaccurate picture of Mauritania to the powerful makers of foreign policy in Washington. Congressional members would have concluded that slavery was dead and that no further investigation or action was necessary. The light that the abolitionists were only just beginning to shine on Mauritania with increasing force would have been extinguished, and a darkness unlike any other would have fallen over that northwestern African nation, blocking its shameful, racist practices from the light of truth.

◈　◈　◈

As the room came alive at the sounding of the gavel, marking the close of the session, I was lost in thought. I was thinking of my ancestors, chained in the holds of those infamous ships, with no one to argue—much less fight—for their release. And I was grateful for the privilege of speaking for their great-great-grandsons and daughters. My joy was tempered, however, by the understanding that a long battle lay ahead of me. Nonetheless, I was buoyed by the realization that I had helped to slow the adversaries' advance and had gained a sympathetic ear in the Congress of the United States.

As I pushed away from the table and turned to walk over to the spectators' section, I saw that my African brothers and sisters were already on their feet and coming toward me. I could feel in their handshakes and see in their eyes that they were very happy. They had their day in Congress. Their voices had reached the highest levels of the U.S. government. Their efforts to make known the suffering of their friends and families was now part of the Congressional record. I could sense their relief from the feeling of powerlessness that must accompany such effort and doubt. They were thinking, "I have not just emigrated from Mauritania to the United States and become comfortable and forgotten my people's plight back home."

They hugged me and said with pride, "Samba Kane, we beat them today, didn't we? The Americans can see now what kind of place Mauritania is, can't they, Samba? Now the world will come to know that slavery exists and that our people have suffered greatly!"

I answered that not only do they see, but the Subcommittee members' reactions indicated that these men and women would take some action. The State Department would have to look much more deeply into this issue and take it much more seriously, I said. This had been a good day, indeed.

◈　　◈　　◈

As we left the hearing room and entered the hallway, a brother approached me and reminded me that Tony Brown had wanted to interview me by telephone immediately after the session. I looked at my watch and noticed that the session had gone past the time I had earlier specified to Brown's producer. I hurried to a telephone booth, but, as I suspected, it was too late. However, the producer told me not to worry. Tony would have me on both his radio and television programs as soon as we could work out the details. I thanked him and thanked Tony for being so supportive on the slavery issue.

◈　　◈　　◈

Upon arriving back in New York, I checked my answering machine. I had received calls from my friends and co-supporters of the anti-slavery movement, Elombe Braith and Samori Marksman. Both had requested that I join them for interviews on their respective radio programs. Irving Manigault of the Harlem-based African Nationalist Pioneer Movement had also called and offered spiritual and financial support. These gestures were much-appreciated and strengthened me for the work that lay ahead.

There was more good news. Soon after the Congressional hearings, U.S. Ambassador to Mauritania Sampas was ordered to open up communications with the indigenous anti-slavery groups. Sampas began to meet with representatives of the Haratine organizations El Hor and SOS-Esclaves as well as with Negro-African groups who were fighting to abolish slavery in Mauritania. The mountains of evidence these dedicated individuals and organizations had been collecting for so many years were finally brought to light.

I also learned later that, as a result of these conferences, Ambassador Sampas interceded to help Aîchanna Boilil regain custody of three of her five children who were held in bondage after her escape, and pressure is being brought to bear for the return of the other two. More importantly, based on these and other findings, including those revealed during the Subcommittee hearings at which I testified, House Resolution 4036-3 was passed by the 104th Congress. This resolution effectively penalizes the Mauritanian government for continuing to support slavery, stating in Section 202 that the U.S. government, effective October 1, 1996:

> ...should not provide economic assistance, military assistance or arms transfers to the Government of Mauritania unless the President certifies to the Congress that such government has taken appropriate action to eliminate chattel slavery in Mauritania including: (1) the enactment of anti-slavery laws that provide appropriate punishment for violators of such laws; and (2) the rigorous enforcement of such laws.

Resolution 4036-3 represents a hard-fought but partial victory for the Mauritanian freedom struggle. Such victories are sweet, but the fight is far from over. There are many forces arrayed against those who seek to put an end to this evil. America's black political and spiritual leaders remain far too silent on the issue, and there is as yet no black grassroots movement in this country that can be mobilized to address the continuing presence of slavery in Mauritania and elsewhere. These vital components of the struggle remain to be put into place. I was committed to seeing that they were.

Still, I breathed a big sigh of relief once the hearings were over and the dust had settled from all the verbal battling with Congressmen and lobbyists and policy wonks. I had done what I set out to do. I had gone to Africa to get the evidence, and that evidence had fueled the powerful engine of truth. It had gotten things rolling.

I had changed on a personal level as well. Whereas before I had seen the task that had initiated all of this activity as simply an assignment, I now saw it as my mission. And far from resting on my laurels, I knew that there was much more for me to do in life than write articles and be done with them.

I had gone to Africa to find a story. I had found that and much, much more. I had found my history. I had found my future. I had found myself.

CHAPTER EIGHT

The only people who accept slavery are the Negroes, owing to their low degree of humanity and their proximity to the animal stage. Other persons who accept the status of slave do so as a means of attaining high rank or power, as is the case with the Mameluk [mamluk] Turks in the east and with those Franks and Galicians who enter the service of the state [in Spain].[1]
—IBN KHALDUN, 1332-1406

Men make their own history, but they do not make it just as they please; they do not make it under circumstances chosen by themselves, but under circumstances directly encountered, given and transmitted from the past. The tradition of all the dead generations weighs like a nightmare on the brain of the living. And just when they seem engaged in revolutionizing themselves and things, in creating something that has never yet existed, precisely in such periods of revolutionary crisis, they anxiously conjure up the spirits of the past to their service and borrow from them names, battle cries and costumes in order to present the new scene of world history in this time-honoured disguise and this borrowed language.[2]
—KARL MARX

I am by nature a conservative man and not given to wild theories. Gaining access to the minds of black people by feeding upon their open wounds with a vile mixture of fact and fiction is unconscionable to me. I detest smooth-talking individuals who spew forth groundless assumptions as much as I hate talented speakers—toxic word magicians, I call them—who rant and rave and believe they must concoct some bubbling, demagogic brew in order to excite blacks to a frenzy. Thus, in plotting my strategy for developing a U.S. mass movement against slavery, I was guided by the words of Frantz Fanon:

> These truths do not have to be hurled in men's faces. They are not intended to ignite fervor. I do not trust fervor. Every time it has burst out somewhere, it has brought fire, famine, misery...and contempt for man. Fervor is the weapon of choice of the impotent. Of those who heat the iron in order to shape it at once. I should prefer to warm a man's body and leave him.[3]

I was not inclined to turn the findings of my research into a sideshow in exchange for fifteen minutes of fame on "Oprah" or "Geraldo." I was not going to race around the country beating people over the head with my information, fudging the facts or distorting the truth, just to get a bigger headline or a longer interview. No, I figured, this story would stand on its own. All I had to do was tell it as I had seen it. The world would beat a path to my door.

It was not to happen.

※　　※　　※

Upon returning to the U.S., I quickly resumed my work organizing a grassroots African-American response to slavery in the Arab world. In that arena, I found myself asking more questions than I was answering.

As I traveled around the country delivering lectures and screening the reels and reels of film I had shot to document black suffering in Mauritania and Senegal, I met few African-Americans who showed any real interest or concern for the topic. A few polite souls would listen patiently, some would even express surprise or anger, but strangely, at least to me, when we met again they would not ask me for more information about what was happening. In fact, they seemed to want to avoid any further discussion of the subject like it was the plague.

Imagine my surprise when I went out to speak in public forums in Harlem and Washington, D.C., and other cities around the U.S., and the turnout of people in general and blacks in particular would be so pitifully low as to be almost embarrassing. Only in Chicago and Milwaukee did any black folks attend my discussions in any significant numbers. Still, their presence was inadequate to generate any substantial African-American involvement in the anti-slavery movement.

This lack of response or interest from a people who, just a little less than two hundred years ago, were themselves chattel slaves baffled me to no end. What did our apathy mean? I wondered. What was at the root of it?

❖ ❖ ❖

I thought about Ibn Khaldun's comments. Was he right? Did black people somehow accept slavery as their lot and by inference accept the fact that slavery would always exist so long as there are black people on this planet? Was this tacit acceptance responsible for African-Americans' apparent lack of interest in the plight of their fellow Africans in Mauritania, Senegal, Sudan, and other parts of the Arab world? Or was their aversion of the issue based on a desire to avoid acknowledging a painful past—a past that my research had revealed was not dead, and that I had seen with my own two eyes was manifesting itself all over again, in all its ugliness, in the present?

The answers to these questions had yet to unfold, but it soon became clear to me that my African-American brothers and sisters had a great deal of soul searching to do before they could sufficiently confront the issue my investigations had uncovered.

I had to do some soul searching of my own to understand the reasons behind this antipathy. I have since drawn many conclusions. First, I concluded that many African-Americans assume that they know all there is to know about slavery. "We know all about how our ancestors were enslaved," they proclaim, "and we know all about the conditions that gave rise to slavery in Europe and the Americas." However, I also realized that what those of us who are the descendants of slaves and who live outside of Africa have never properly addressed is the question of why our predecessors were enslaved on such a grand scale.

Beyond that, there is the twin issue of complacency and nonvigilance. We blacks in the West believe that we are so well placed that the nightmare of chattel slavery cannot possibly raise its ugly head to threaten us again. We erroneously believe that slavery died on a worldwide scale with the Emancipation Proclamation.

That is exactly the kind of mistake that the Jews in Nazi Germany made during World War II. They believed that they were Germans and part of the community of Germans. They bought into the rhetoric that Germany was a civilized nation and that such monstrous behavior as the incarceration and incineration of human beings simply because they worshipped their Creator in a particular way was impossible. They were loyal to "their" country. They believed that Herr Hitler and their Aryan countrymen and women would never turn on them to the vile degree that did inevitably did.

But they were wrong, and six million Jews perished to prove it. As a result, most Jewish people today hold no illusions that another holocaust could possibly not happen again. That is why they are today among the most vigilant of the world's people for even the slightest signs of Nazism's and fascism's recurring evils.

But the Jews have not been subjected to anywhere near the devastation that African people have collectively endured and continue to endure. We lost far more than six million people in our holocaust. We lost hundreds of millions more in the slave trade. Yet when we are presented with evidence of the enduring legacy of African slavery, we avert our eyes to keep from seeing the horrible specter of our past. We cover our ears to keep from hearing the truth.

What is wrong with us?

❖   ❖   ❖

Legal historian and analyst Derrick Bell has shared some arresting insights that relate to the personal and political implications of African-Americans' antipathy about modern-day slavery in their ancestral homeland. According to Bell:

> When I was growing up in the years before the Second World War, our slave heritage was more a symbol of shame than a source of pride. It burdened black people with an indelible mark of difference as we struggled to be like whites. In those far-off days, survival and progress seemed to require moving beyond, even rejecting slavery....In those days, self-delusion was both easy and comforting....We sang spirituals but detached the songs from their slave origins.
>
> As I look back, I see this reaction as no less sad for being very understandable. We were a subordinate and mostly shunned portion of a society that managed to lay the onus of slavery neatly on those who were slaves while simultaneously exonerating those who were slaveholders. All things considered, it seemed a history best left alone.[4]

These and other conclusions I added to my own experiences as I struggled to propel the American anti-slavery movement forward. They confirmed my suspicion that many African-Americans' professed (and often new-found) love for and pride in Africa and their African heritage is a fantasy. So many are so mired in the African past that they overlook the realities of the African present. By doing so, however, they avoid addressing those realities.

Each year, for example, hundreds of black Americans visit the infamous island of Gorée in Senegal, from which many of their ancestors began the painful voyage to enslavement. Yet just a short distance north of Gorée are villages and refugee camps that provide sanctuary to tens of thousands of blacks who have run away to escape slavery in Mauritania, some of them as recently as a few months ago.

❀   ❀   ❀

Upon my return to the U.S., I realized that too few African-Americans possess a really firm or clear understanding of the contemporary African political, social, and cultural landscape. Nor are they aware of the incredible kinds of suffering and debasement that African people continue to endure in their homelands. Thus, insofar as the issue of the continuing slavery in northwestern Africa is concerned, most African-Americans cannot be expected to instantaneously connect the Abid or the Haratine experiences to their own in any concrete way. I also concluded that most African-Americans have never really come to hate the *institution* of slavery for its own sake. They only hate what it has done to African-Americans as a subgroup within the African Diaspora, and they turn a deaf ear to instances of slavery that do not directly affect them or their families.

Derrick Bell is right on target when he comments about the implications of this kind of thinking:

> ... [T]he fact of slavery refuses to fade, along with the deeply
> embedded personal attitudes and public policy assumptions that
> supported it for so long. Indeed, the racism that made slavery fea-
> sible is far from dead in the last decade of twentieth century
> America; and the civil rights gains, so hard won, are being steadi-
> ly eroded.[5]

Similarly, Bell's conclusions about American whites are certainly applicable to African Arabs, who continue to practice and/or support the enslavement of black people in Africa, when he states that "slavery is an example of what white America has done, [and] a constant reminder of what white America might do."[6]

The question, then, it seems to me, is a simple one: Should we, the descendants of slaves, ignore the sins of one group of slavers and slaveholders—namely, the Arabs of northwestern Africa today—while pointing out and chastising those of another—that is, the ancestors of our white American compatriots?

I for one choose not to let either one off the hook. Slavery is slavery, and slavery is wrong—no matter who engages in it. But how was I to involve my African-American countrymen and countrywomen in the fight for the freedom of our brothers and sisters in Mauritania, Senegal, and Sudan, who are literally our brothers and sisters who were never freed? And I'm not, for the sake of making my point, stretching the truth when I say this.

It's true. My research had shown me that many of the Africans who were crammed into the hulls of those infamous slave ships were captured from the coastal areas of what presently comprises Mauritania, Senegal, and Sudan. As Joseph E. Holloway reports in his book, Africanisms in American Culture:

> *Between 1670 and 1700, Africans were imported to South Carolina predominantly from "Guinea." The majority of these "Guinea" Africans were Wolofs and other Mandes, such as Bambaras, Fulani, and Susus. The Wolofs, the most numerous of the African groups to arrive in the United States in the seventeenth century, were mostly house servants....Around 1670, the Wolof, or Jolof, empire broke up into a number of kingdoms owing to a revolt instigated by Mauritanian Marabouts [Arab-Berber holy men].[7]*

These "Guinea Africans" were the ancestors of the very people whom I had lived among and interviewed in my effort to document the continuing existence of slavery! There is a direct connection between the Mauritanian Abid and Haratines and Negro-Africans on one side of the Atlantic Ocean, and the African-American South Carolinians and Georgians and Kentuckians and so forth on the other!

How much more "real" would I have to make this issue before black people in the United States could grab hold of it?

❖ ❖ ❖

Early in this struggle, no black newspapers or radio and television stations were interested in covering the story my investigation had confirmed with the professionalism and in-depth coverage that it deserved. Instead, black journalists were notorious for allowing themselves to be wined and dined and toured around by the very governments guilty of committing these atrocities. They would then return to the U.S. to write glowing reports about these governments and their puppet or autocratic leaders.

Remember the infamous black press junkets to Uganda during the reign of Idi Amin Dada? Those "brother" and "sister" reporters came home and told us that everything was fine in Uganda. Only years later did we find out that something was rotten in Africa.

Until the white media—for reasons of its own—latched onto Muslim Minister Louis Farrakhan's denial of the existence of slavery after his trips to northern Africa in 1996, escaped slaves and refugees from Mauritania and the Sudan could not get an appearance on black media programs. But the white press wasn't concerned about slavery, either. Their target was Minister Farrakhan, who generally avoided the subject. This fascinated media analysts, who made a lot of noise over the fact that, despite compelling evidence to the contrary, the most prominent black leader of our time showed no interest in the enslavement of black people on the continent of Africa and actually denied its existence. They hounded Farrakhan with questions about his views on the issue, and he had no qualms about showing his displeasure with their probing.

It was Minister Farrakhan's persistent negations and apparent apathy that gave the anti-slavery movement its greatest media boost. On the December 10, 1996, episode of the NBC television program "Dateline," he finally blew his top. "If slavery exists," he angrily rebutted, "why don't *you* go, as a member of the press, and look inside of the Sudan! And if you find it, then you come back and tell the American people what you found!"

Again, Farrakhan held true to the Nation of Islam's practice of focusing on and protecting the image of Sudan, while skillfully evading the issue of slavery in Mauritania. To this day, Nation of Islam spokesmen have never admitted that slavery exists in either nation. They have, however, acknowledged the racism and mistreatment of blacks there, while holding fast to the rationale that the allegations of slavery are part of a Jewish plot to separate blacks and Arabs.

◈　◈　◈

In the last few years since becoming involved in this issue, I have met with the heads of various black Orthodox Muslim organizations who have appeared to be both sympathetic and cautious in their approach to the subject of slavery in the Arab world. Their concern was sincere, but they have never initiated any action to address the issue. They have never been threatening or obstructing, but they have perhaps been more concerned about the image of Islam to be of any assistance or support to the anti-slavery movement. Torn between loyalty to Islam and their perception of themselves as black people, they have placed their religion above the liberation of their fellow man. As a result, they too have shown no interest in helping to eliminate this plague upon the homeland of their ancestors.

The silence on this issue of those in the Islamic world, particularly black Muslims, both those in Africa and the United States, is disturbing. The silence of white orthodox Muslims sends the message that race rules the relationships among blacks and whites within Islam just as it continues to rule those between blacks and whites in Christendom. Yet, if a sufficient number of blacks who worship Islam make enough noise, even if it has to be done behind closed doors, the criminal activity that is happening in Mauritania and Sudan can come to a halt.

Were it not for the courage of Tony Brown and of Andrew Cooper of the *City Sun*, of human rights activist Elombe Braith, of radio personalities Samori Marksman and Utrice Leid of Pacifica Radio station WBAI-FM in New York City, news of this modern-day holocaust and its accompanying human suffering would never have reached the light of day. These people and their organizations are really heroes. Yet despite their example, the black media, by and large, has been resistant to giving this issue the kind of attention it needs and merits.

◈   ◈   ◈

Even more shameful has been the ignorance and apathy of America's black leaders. Black politicians, church leaders, and other influential personalities have done little to educate the African-American or wider public on this matter. Most do not see it as important enough to place on their agendas. For example, my organization, CASMAS, has repeatedly sent material documenting the existence of slavery in northwestern Africa to Jesse Jackson, head of the Rainbow Coalition. So far, however, Jackson has refused to give a statement, and his aides have informed me that he does not foresee a time when he will be able to address the issue, given his commitments to other causes.

My experience testifying before the Congressional subcommittee showed me that knowledge of slavery in Africa and the Arab slave trade is common knowledge in U.S. political circles. So far, only a handful of African-Americans in Congress have raised their voices and gone on record to speak out consistently against the injustices that are being committed against Africans in the Arab world. Congressman Donald Payne of New Jersey is one of these. Since 1994, Payne has fought an uphill battle to get his colleagues in the Congressional Black Caucus to address this issue. Representative Eleanor Holmes Norton, Washington, D.C.'s nonvoting delegate to Congress, is another. She recently joined with Representatives Barney Frank (D-NJ) and Frank Torriccelli (D-NJ) to co-sponsor HR-49, House Resolution Number 49, a bill that would require the United States to take action against human bondage.

While not explicitly condemning Mauritania or Sudan, HR-49 would make the eradication of slavery an "important goal for the U.S. Government in all of its activities." It would direct the Secretary of State to include in the State Department's annual human rights report "a full report on slavery wherever it exists throughout the world." It would also require the U.S., in cooperation with regional organizations and the United Nations, to "draw up a multinational plan to put an end to slavery wherever it exists throughout the world" by the year 2000.

Referring to the American experience of slavery, Norton has stated that our nation's history commands that it lead the way in these efforts. Unfortunately, passage of this important resolution has been stalled in the Congress until now, but members of the American abolitionist movement are currently preparing an initiative to revive it.

Despite Norton's and Payne's efforts, most of the heavy-duty fighting at the Congressional level to put pressure on the United States to end slavery in Africa is being carried out by white Republicans—Christopher Smith (R-NJ), Dick Zimmer (R-NJ), and Frank Wolf (R-VA), to name a few. Smith, the Chair of the House Subcommittee on International Operations and Human Rights, has publicly voiced his disappointment over the lack of interest of black politicians on the slavery issue. In July 1993, Congressman Wolf wrote a letter to Benjamin Chavis, then-executive director of the NAACP, requesting that organization's support in condemning the Sudanese government for its refusal to stop the practice of slavery in that country. Wolf's letter was frank and to the point:

> *Most recently, I received a copy of a very disturbing State Department cable containing reliable information that in Sudan, human rights abuses such as kidnapping, slavery and the export of women and children from southern and central Sudan are escalating dramatically, despite the denials and rhetoric from Sudanese government officials....I hope that you will speak out against the continuing cruelty which has caused the people of Sudan so much pain and suffering. The efforts of the NAACP could be the difference between life and death for millions of people.*[8]

Chavis did not respond. Representative Wolf wrote him again a month later:

> *Since I last wrote to you, thousands more in southern Sudan have died. Please let me know if the NAACP is willing to step forward. Please let me know if you will personally become involved. This is not an easy task, but the combined efforts of many Americans...could result in saving the lives of tens of thousands of innocent people.*[9]

There would be no response to this letter, nor to a similar plea sent to Randall Robinson, executive director of TransAfrica, that same day. The NAACP later showed some indication of entering this struggle, however, if but only slightly. And then only as the result of the bold activism of a longtime member and director of its Detroit, Michigan branch: Mr. Joseph Madison.

In July 1995, I spoke to Mr. Madison, whose TPT Network is a syndicate service that works with black talk radio stations in Atlanta, Chicago, Detroit, Philadelphia, and six other cities. Madison had his own radio talk show in Detroit and had hosted a show in Washington, D.C. years ago. A member of the NAACP since age twenty-one, the forty-five-year-old Madison had, like me, first learned about the ongoing problems of slavery in Africa from "Tony Brown's Journal."

Madison was very interested in pursuing the issue. He had conducted interviews with individuals representing various abolitionist groups, notably with Charles Jacobs. During my interview on his Detroit radio program, I brought to his attention the letters that Congressman Wolf had sent to Ben Chavis. Madison informed me that he had no knowledge of such letters. The issue had never come before the NAACP executive board, he claimed, and he would have known, being that he was a member of it.

On the air, Madison gave me his word that he would present a resolution to the NAACP asking the organization to take a strong stand against slavery in Africa. And if they did not accept it, he declared, he would resign. He would be risking twenty-four years of service, he said, but he was clear on the issue and firmly set on his course.

True to his word, Madison drafted a resolution and showed it to the NAACP board chairperson, Mrs. Myrlie Evers-Williams, prior to introducing it. The resolution specifically condemned "the barbaric practice of slavery and...the mass expulsions and slaughter" in Mauritania and Sudan. Echoing Delegate Norton's comments, it further stated that the NAACP, "whose members, in part, are descendants of slaves, recognizes that our own history commands that we act on behalf of those held in human bondage. We now come to the front line of this struggle and we will not rest until these slaves are freed."

Evers-Williams was overwhelmingly supportive and promised to give the initiative her full backing. The resolution was presented at the board's May 20, 1996, meeting. Here's Madison's take on that session:

> The meeting was a very, very difficult one. The organization's financial situation was bleak. There had been a changing of the guard. As you know, Myrlie Evers-Williams had been selected to replace Ben Chavis, and she won by only one vote. But when this issue came forth, it got the immediate attention of everyone. People stopped caucusing, they stopped talking amongst themselves. They were really listening. People who were knowledgeable about it spoke up and said, "Look, this slavery thing has got to stop!" We had youth council chapter presidents who came forth and requested additional information to take back to their universities. In unison, everybody put aside their differences and voted in favor of this resolution. When it was introduced, it received a round of applause from everyone in the room, especially those from the Washington, D.C., bureau office, who immediately began spreading the word to their Congressional colleagues about the NAACP's position.

I was overjoyed to hear this news. Nevertheless, the NAACP has yet to commit itself to any definitive course of action against the Mauritanian or Sudanese governments. "We're talking a lot, and we're still in the process of analyzing the situation and ferreting out the facts," claimed Earl Shinhoster, the organization's current acting executive director, when I spoke with him recently. As he further explained, "It is a situation that is ripe for emotion, but not a situation that can be advocated purely on emotion. I do think all points of view need to be put on the table, and the American people, as a whole, need to take a more urgent view of this situation."[10]

※　※　※

This lack of a concerted response from establishment black organizations and their leadership has led me to believe that, in the end, a grassroots movement of African-Americans will have to rise up and stand at the forefront of this issue. The black man and woman on the street are the African slave's only hope of forcing America's black and other political and spiritual leaders to voice moral outrage over the injustices and barbarism of trading in black flesh. They will be the ones to knock down the blood-and suffering-soaked walls of silence and indifference that surround this ongoing travesty of inhumanity. I believe now more than ever in the credo which states that "Evil exists when good people do nothing." Our leaders will never address the issue unless a grassroots movement lights a fire beneath them.

And that is exactly what we must do. This struggle will require commitment and dedication. It will require effort and determination. Those of us who engage in it will meet with stonewalling and lies, resistance and deceit, false friends and unscrupulous enemies who will stop at nothing to keep from losing the privileges that racism and the ownership of others has afforded them. This struggle is not one that we are going to win overnight, but we must persevere.

For black people in the U.S. and others outside of Africa, it is both a personal *and* a political battle. I am involved because I hate the institution of slavery and the almost irreparable damage and pain it visits on helpless human beings. I resist slavery because not to resist it would be to lose my humanity. My research, my associations with those who are working to rid the world of chattel slavery, my travels to Africa, my encounters living and learning among those who suffer and those who are fighting and dying to end that suffering have taught me many things. These people and experiences have changed my mind and reshaped my consciousness.

※　※　※

Yesterday, I was a student and a freelance reporter. Today, I am a freedom fighter and a spokesperson for a cause. Yesterday, I was ignorant and confused. Today, my vision is clear. Yesterday, I saw this issue in black and white, as one of Arab versus African, Christian versus Muslim. Today, I believe that help with this anti-slavery movement will come from people of all races, colors, and faiths—from anyone who has the goodness of heart to tell the difference between right and wrong, no matter who commits the injustice.

I place my hope in those who hate injustice in every form it takes, who owe no allegiance to a particular religious or political belief. People who are brothers and sisters of the spirit because they hear the call to correct an evil and are compelled to answer it. I welcome their help.

Are you one of those people?

CHAPTER NINE

M*an is mortal. That may be; but let us die resisting, and if our lot
is complete annihilation, let us not behave in such a way that it
seems justice!*[1]
—ALBERT CAMUS

There is much that you can do if you want to take a stand in the struggle to eliminate slavery in northwestern Africa. The following are just a few
suggestions to get your involvement in this grassroots movement rolling:

1. Raise the issue of the chattel enslavement of black Africans in
   Mauritania, Sudan, and elsewhere in the Arab world at every international forum and event you attend.

2. Join or create organizations of persons who are concerned about
   the continued presence of slavery in the world. Form linkages
   with other human rights and anti-slavery organizations here in
   the United States and elsewhere.

3. Write your Congresspersons and other state and local officials
   and ask them to put pressure on the executive and legislative
   branches of government to demand that Mauritania and Sudan
   abide by the United Nations conventions, international law, and
   other international treaties to which they are party. Specifically,
   these sanctions include:

(a) Article 4 of the 1948 Universal Declaration of Human Rights, which specifically outlaws slavery and servitude in all their forms;

(b) the 1951 Convention for the Suppression of the Traffic in Persons and of the Exploitation and Prostitution of Others;

(c) the 1957 Supplementary Convention on the Abolition of Slavery, the Slave Trade, and Institutions and Practices Similar to Slavery; and

(d) the 1981 African Charter on Human and Peoples' Rights.

4. Oppose federal, World Bank, and other international loans and grants to Mauritania and Sudan, except those that address humanitarian needs, until the practice of chattel slavery is abolished and black African refugees from these two nations are permitted to return.

5. Demand that United Nations agencies, specifically the U.N. High Commission on Refugees and World Food Program, continue to provide humanitarian aid to Mauritanian refugees living in camps in Senegal and Mali until they are able to return home with guarantees of security.

6. Demand that the United Nations launch an independent investigation into the gross abuses of human rights in Mauritania and Sudan—notably the deportations and massacres of black Africans from 1989 to 1991 and the military occupation of the Senegal River Valley—and bring to justice those responsible.

7. Demand that the legal status of independent human rights and anti-slavery organizations operating in Mauritania and Sudan be recognized, and insist that these groups be allowed to conduct their own fact-finding investigations into the status of slavery and slaves in these countries.

8. Demand that the Mauritanian and Sudanese governments each issue a single national law on slavery that:

(a) provides specific definitions of the terms "slavery," "slave," "slave trader," and "slaveholder" in their national contexts;

(b) makes slavery a crime, and

(c) stipulates penalties for those who engage in slavery.

9. Demand that the Mauritanian and Sudanese governments immediately issue public proclamations and mount large-scale public
information campaigns attesting to the illegality of slavery.
These announcements should be issued via the local and national media in every language spoken by the people of the two nations. In addition, official documents should be sent to local
government authorities instructing them to arrest and try any
person who breaches the law by trading or holding slaves. Further, curricula should be implemented in Mauritanian and Sudanese schools that educate Arab and African students about
human rights and the eradication of slavery.

10. Demand that international pressure be brought to bear upon
the Mauritanian government to acknowledge the expulsion of
black Mauritanians into Senegal and Mali, and insist that these
refugees be permitted to return to their homeland under conditions of security and dignity, including the return of or compensation for their land, belongings, and employment.

11. Demand that the Mauritanian and Sudanese governments initiate programs that give freed slaves equal access to land, paid
employment, economic and social opportunity, and education.
Freed blacks should be permitted to move freely about within
these nations without fear of arbitrary re-enslavement, arrest,
or harassment.

12. Demand that the Mauritanian and Sudanese government create
agencies, similar to the Freedman's Bureau that operated in
the United States after the Civil War, to oversee the development of equitable economic, social, and political conditions for
freed slaves.

13. Write to the governments and diplomatic officials of other
African nations, asking them to explain their silence and apparent lack of sensitivity to the fate of their fellow Africans
in Mauritania and Sudan. Demand that these nations take
a stand either by supporting the anti-slavery movements within these nations or by supporting sanctions against the two
countries.

14. Write to the governments and diplomatic officials of Islamic

nations, to Muslim and Arab organizations, and/or to inter-faith groups in the United States and abroad, asking them to do the same.

WORDS TO NEW WORLD AFRICANS

W*hen that which was done in the dark is brought into the light, when evils are exposed, such as those related to slavery, invariably the character of those who grasp the horrors of the revelation are tested. It is easy to rant and rage against horrors lost in antiquity, to express bitterness and anger for those tortured souls now asleep in death, or to shake one's fists at ghosts. The difficulty lies in opposing a living adversary whose rapacious appetites are hell-bound to decimate all that one holds dear in the here and now.*

It is a profound experience when your adversary confronts you in battle. When the plunderer points to his spoils and hurls a challenge that finds its mark in the very center of your being: "Yes, I did it! Now what are you going to do about it?" It is then that you must look deep inside yourself and bring forth a response that puts an end to the rivalry. That silences the foe. That squashes the threat.

What will be done about slavery in Africa today?

History rarely gives us a chance to confront a tormentor previously lost to time and place. Are there not others of my African-American brothers and sisters who have, like me, fantasized about traveling back in time to prevent the rape of our ancestral homeland, Mother Africa? Or of leading the charge of unbound African warriors, up from the hold of the slave ship Zion, to slay the enslavers on its deck and emancipate its terrified cargo?

Well, a window in time has reopened. Now what are we going to do about it?

The modern-day curse of slavery in Mauritania and Sudan presents us simultaneously with a challenge and a blessing—indeed, an opportunity to end this madness, once and for all. Will we African-Americans continue to do as we have done in the past? Will we play down the role being played by the Arabs in supporting and extending the vile trade in black flesh? Will we exonerate them while turning a baleful gaze on more familiar conspirators or on newly discovered ones? Will we point solely to the White "Christian soldiers" who perpetrated the Middle Passage. Or will we singularly chastise a few dead Jewish merchants who financed and profited from it?

Will those of us who follow Islam take action to rise up and reprove their Islamic kin who even today enslave fellow Muslims or turn a blind eye to enslavement simply because the skin color of the oppressed is different from that of their own?

Will a moan of anguish and a shout of solidarity rumble across the Atlantic from those of us who sit in the pews of black Christian churches every Sunday?

Will those of us in leadership positions—those who stand at the helm of organizations that in the past have been quite vocal about slavery, apartheid, and racial injustice—be seen in the first charges of this battle?

What will we do about this issue of slavery, not that which we know of in the past, but that which still exists on African soil today?

In the final analysis, each and every one of us must examine the evidence with our hearts and with our consciences and decide where we stand on this issue.

Whether you choose to close your eyes and ignore it, preferring instead to shake your fists at the ghosts of the distant past—or whether you decide to join the ranks of the modern-day abolitionist movement and add your voice to others joined in protest—one thing is clear: until the enslavement of African men women and children vanishes from the face of this earth forever, this discussion will go on.

CHAPTER NOTES

◆ CHAPTER NOTES ◆

Prologue

1 David Diop, "Le Temps du Martyre," in Léopold Sédar Senghor, ed., *Anthologie de la Nouvelle Poésie Nègre et Malgache de Langue Française* (Paris: Presses Universitaires de France, 1977), 174.

Chapter 1

1 Letter from the Honorable Ronald V. Dellums (D–California) to His Excellency Maaouya Ould Sid Ahmed Taya, President of Mauritania, 23 April 1991.

2 Quoted in Janet Fleishman, *Mauritania's Campaign of Terror: State-Sponsored Repression of Black Africans* (New York: Human Rights Watch/Africa, 1994), 26. This report is based on the author's three fact-finding missions to Senegal (May–June 1990, February– March 1991, and October–November 1993) as well as numerous interviews she conducted in Paris, New York, and Washington, D.C. Human Rights Watch/Africa is a nongovernmental organization established in 1988 to monitor and promote the observance of internationally recognized human rights in Africa.

3 Tony Brown Productions, Inc., "Tony Brown's Journal" (Show Number 1909: "A First-Hand View of Slavery in Africa"). A videotape of this show can be ordered from Tony Brown Productions by calling (212) 575-0876.

4 Fleishman, *Mauritania's Campaign of Terror*, 79.

5 Garba Diallo, "Mauritania: The Other Apartheid?" *Current African Issues*, 16 (February 1993): 14–15.

6 Ibn Khaldun, quoted in Diallo, "Mauritania: The Other Apartheid?": 15.

7 Ernest Gellner and Charles Michaud, eds., *Arabs and Berbers* (Lexington, MA: Lexington Books, 1972); Robert Montagne, *The Berbers: Their Social and Political Organization*, trans. David Seddon (London: F. Cass, 1973).

8 Diallo, "Mauritania: The Other Apartheid?": 14–15.

9 Ibid., 15.

10 Ibid., 40.

11 Fleishman, *Mauritania's Campaign of Terror*, 82.

12 Ibid., 8.

13 Amnesty International, *Mauritania 1986–1989: Background to a Crisis—Three Years of Political Imprisonment, Torture and Unfair Trials* (New York: Amnesty International, November 1989), 11.

14 Ibid., 23.

15 Fleishman, *Mauritania's Campaign of Terror*, 115.

16 Ibid., 115.

17 Ibid.

18 Interview with Mamadou Bocar Ba, in Dakar, Senegal, on 23 December 1996, conducted by the author. Mamadou's testimony is supported in detail by interviews conducted by Human Rights Watch/Africa (see Fleishman, *Mauritania's Campaign of Terror*, 14-17); see also Diallo, "Mauritania: The Other Apartheid?": 10-11, 42.

19 Fleishman, *Mauritania's Campaign of Terror*, 14.

20 Garba Diallo, *Indigenous Forms of Learning in Africa* (Report Number 7) (Oslo: University of Oslo, 1994), 26.

21 Diallo, "Mauritania: The Other Apartheid?": 10, 11.

22 Fleishman, *Mauritania's Campaign of Terror*, 18.

23 Ibid., 19.

24 Audiotaped interview with a Lutheran worker in N'Dioum refugee camp on 26 December 1995, conducted by the author. Interview is featured in the videodocumentary, *Mauritania and the Arab Slave Trade 1996*, produced by the author and available through CASMAS (the Coalition Against Slavery in Mauritania and Sudan). CASMAS can be reached at (212) 774-4287.

25 Fleishman, *Mauritania's Campaign of Terror*, 29.

26 "Mauritania: More than 200 Black Political Detainees Executed or Tortured to Death," *News From Africa Watch* (31 May 1991): 1.

27 Diallo, *Indigenous Forms of Learning in Africa*, 26.

28 Fleishman, *Mauritania's Campaign of Terror*, 65.

29 Ibid.

30 Ibid., 68.

31 Diallo, *Indigenous Forms of Learning in Africa*, 27.

32 Interviews with Mauritanian refugees Mansour Kane and El Hadj Demba Ba conducted by the author in New York City, November/December 1996.

33 Thurston Clarke, *The Last Caravan* (New York: Putnam, 1978); Peter Fuchs, *The Land of Veiled Men* (New York: Citadel Press, 1956); Jeremy Keenan, *The Tuareg: People of Ahaggar* (New York: St. Martin's Press, 1978); H. T. Norris, *The Tuareg: Their Islamic Legacy and Its Diffusion in the Sahel* (Warminster: Aris & Phillips, 1975); Francis James Rennell Rodd, *The People of the Veil* (London: Macmillan, 1926); Jan Reynolds, *Sahara: Vanishing Cultures* (San Diego: Harcourt Brace Jovanovich, 1991).

34 U.S. Department of State, "Prohibition of Forced or Compulsory Labor," in U.S. Department of State, *Country Reports on Human Rights Practices for 1994* (Washington, D.C.: U.S. Department of State, 1995), 166.

35 Diallo, "Mauritania: The Other Apartheid?": 20, 21.

36 Chancellor Williams was cited without a page reference in Edward Scobie, *The Moors and Portugal's Global Expansion* (Occasional Paper Number 12) (New York: Department of Black Studies, City College of the City University of New York, 1996), 2.

37 Diallo, "Mauritania: The Other Apartheid?": 20, 21.

38 Alfred Gerteiny, *Mauritania* (London: Pall Mall Press Limited, 1967), 60.

Chapter 2

1 Quoted in Simon Sebag Montefiore, "Black Market," *Sunday [London] Times Magazine* (17 November 1996): 36-44. Montefiore conducted an undercover investigation of slavery in Mauritania. See also Elinor Burkett, "God Created Me to Be a Slave," *New York Times Magazine* (12 October 1997): 56–60. Burkett's article describes the sexual abuse of slaves and the long-term of effects of slavery in Mauritania.

2 Thomas K. Park, Mamadou Baro, and Tidiane Ngaido, *Conflicts Over Land and the Crisis of Nationalism in Mauritania* (Madison, WI: University of Wisconsin Land Tenure Center, 1991), 4, 5.

3 Ibid, 46.

4 Ibid, 5.

5 Rod Nordland, "Slavery," *Newsweek International* (4 May 1992): 32. *Newsweek International* is the English-language version of *Newsweek* magazine that is published in the United States and sold internationally. An abridged presentation of

this article appears in the U.S.-circulation version of the magazine of the same date, with different pagination.

6 Fleishman, *Mauritania's Campaign of Terror*, 86.

7 Ibid.

8 Statement by Boubacar Messaoud, president of SOS–Esclaves, presented at the twenty-first session of the United Nations Economic and Social Council Commission on Human Rights Sub-Commission on Prevention of Discrimination and Protection of Minorities, Working Group on Contemporary Forms of Slavery (Geneva, Switzerland, 21–27 June 1996), 2.

9 Ibid., 3.

10 Ibid., 2.

11 Fleishman, *Mauritania's Campaign of Terror*, 82, 83.

12 Ibid, 83.

13 Statement by Boubacar Messroud, 2.

14 Ibid., 1.

15 Fleishman, *Mauritania's Campaign of Terror*, 80.

16 Ibid., 88, 89

17 Nordland, "Slavery": 32.

18 Fleishman, *Mauritania's Campaign of Terror*, 91.

19 Ibid., 91.

20 Human Rights Watch/Africa, Mauritania—*Slavery: Alive and Well, 10 Years After it was Last Abolished* (New York: Human Rights Watch/Africa, 1990), 15.

21 Fleishman, *Mauritania's Campaign of Terror*, 92.

22 Ibid., 91.

23 Jesse Washington, "Of Human Bondage," *Vibe* (November 1996): 102.

24 Davis quotes from his own work in his review article, "At the Heart of Slavery," published in the *New York Review of Books* (17 October 1996): 52. He is referring to Karl Jacoby's article, "Slaves by Nature? Domestic Animals and Human Slaves," *Slavery & Abolition: A Journal of Slave and Post-Slave Studies*, 15 (April 1994): 89–99. See also David Brion Davis, *Slavery and Human Progress* (New York: Oxford University Press, 1984).

25 Washington, "Of Human Bondage": 102.

26 Fleishman, *Mauritania's Campaign of Terror*, 90.

27 Orlando Patterson, *Slavery and Social Death: A Comparative Study* (Cambridge, MA: Harvard University Press, 1982), 96.

28 Stanley M. Elkins, *Slavery: A Problem in American Institutional and Intellectual Life* (Chicago: The University of Chicago Press, 1959), cited in Patterson, Slavery and Social Death, 96. See also Burkett, "God Created Me To Be A Slave."

29 Davis, "At the Heart of Slavery": 52.

30 Fleishman, *Mauritania's Campaign of Terror*, 90.

31 Ibid., 86. Interview in Senegal, May-June 1990.

32 Ibid., 87. Interview in Senegal, May-June 1990.

33 Ibid., 90-91.

34 Garba Diallo, "They Live in Slavery," *Djembe*, 12 (April–June, 1995): 14.

35 Ibid., 15.

36 Ibid., 17.

Chapter 3

1 John Laffin, *The Arabs as Master Slavers* (Englewood, NJ: SBS Publishing, 1982), 58.

2 Bernard Lewis, *Race and Color in Islam* (New York: Harper & Row, 1971), 5.

3 Ibid., 7.

4 Ibid., 7.

5 Ibid., 10, 11.

6 Philip K. Hitti, *The Arabs: A Short History* (Washington, D.C.: Regnery, 1996), 72–77.

7 Lewis, *Race and Color in Islam*, 10, 11.

8 Ibid, 11.

9 Ibid, 13.

10 Nordland, "Slavery": 32.

11 Lewis, Race and Color in Islam, 23.

12 Ibid., 26.

13 Ibid.

14 Bernard Lewis, *Race and Slavery in the Middle East: An Historical Enquiry* (New York: Oxford University Press, 1990), 52. See also John Ralph Willis, ed., *Slaves and Slavery in Muslim Africa, Volume I: Islam and the Ideology of Enslavement* (London: F. Cass, 1985), 68–69.

15 Quoted in Lewis, *Race and Slavery in the Middle East*, 52.

16 Ibid., 53.

17 Quoted in Murray Gordon, *Slavery in the Arab World* (New York: New Amsterdam, 1989), 102-103.

18 Lewis, *Race and Color in Islam*, 28, 29.

19 Rory Nugent, "March of the Green Flag," *Spin*, (May 1995): 83.

20 Ibid.

21 Claud Anderson, *Black Labor, White Wealth: The Search for Power and Economic Justice* (Edgewood, MD: Duncan & Duncan, 1994), 77.

22 Herbert Gerbeau, "The African Slave Trade from the Fifteenth to the Nineteenth Century," in UNESCO, *Reports and Papers of the Meeting of Experts* (Port-au-Prince, Haiti, 31 January to 4 February 1978) (New York: UNESCO, 1978), 190–92.

23 Ibid., 190, 191.

24 David Brion Davis, quoted in Anderson, Black Labor, White Wealth, 70.

25 Anderson, *Black Labor, White Wealth*, 110.

26 Ibid., 109-110.

27 Thomas Sowell, *Race and Culture: A World View* (New York: Basic Books, 1994), 208.

28 Gordon, *Slavery in the Arab World*, 80–81.

29 Abdullahi Mahadi, "The Aftermath of the Jihad in the Central Sudan as a Major Factor in the Volume of the Trans-Saharan Slave Trade in the Nineteenth Century," *Slavery and Abolition*, 125.

30 Ibid.

31 Ibid.

32 Laffin, *The Arabs as Master Slavers*, 75.

33 Ibid.

34 Ibid.

35 Ibid., 75, 76.

36 Ibid., 76.

37 Ibid.

38 Gordon, *Slavery in the Arab World*, 80–81.

39 Ibid., 84.

40 Ibid., 94–95.
41 Ibid., 92.
42 Ibid., 96.
43 Ibid., 95–96.
44 Mahadi, "The Aftermath of the Jihad": 126.
45 Bernard Lewis, *Race and Color in Islam*, 68.
46 Gordon, *Slavery in the Arab World*, 97.

Chapter 4

1 Friedrich Nietzsche, *Twilight of the Idols/The Anti-Christ* (New York: Viking Penguin, 1987), 26.
2 The articles were published as a four-part series under the heading, "Arab Masters—Black Slaves" and subtitled "The African Slave Trade 1995," "Sorrow and Shame: Brutal N. African Slave Trade Ignored and Denied," "The Slavery Issue: A Crisis in Black Leadership," and "Demographics and the Modern-Day Slave Trade." For copies, contact the Coalition Against Slavery in Mauritania and Sudan (CASMAS) at (212) 774-4287 because the City Sun Publishing Company no longer exists.
3 Gilles Kepel, *Allah in the West: Islamic Movements in America and Europe*, trans. Susan Milner (Stanford, CA: Stanford University Press, 1997), 61.
4 Yusef Salaam, "U.S. Muslims Remain Silent on Sudan Slavery Issue," *New York Amsterdam News* (15 July 1995): 2.
5 Interview with Messaoud Ould Boulkheir, president of El Hor, in Mauritania, January 1996. Boulkheir supplied the author with a case history, contract, and photograph of Koumba Mint Sagheir and her daughter Kneiba.
6 Malcolm X (with the assistance of Alex Haley), *The Autobiography of Malcolm X* (New York: Grove Press, 1965), 345–46.
7 Nordland, "Slavery": 32.
8 Diallo, "Mauritania: The Other Apartheid?": 38.
9 Jesse Washington, "Of Human Bondage": 102.
10 Ibid., 103.

Chapter 5

1 Jacques Roumain, "Bois-d'Ebe'ne" [Prelude], in Léopold Sédar Senghor, ed., *Anthologie de la Nouvelle Poésie Nègre et Malgache de Langue Française* (Paris: Presses Universitaires de France, 1977), 113.
2 Fleishman, *Mauritania's Campaign of Terror*, 84. Interview in Senegal, 1 June 1990.
3 Boubacar Joseph Ndiaye, *The Slave House of Gorée–Island*, trans. Momar Khary Diagne, (no publication information noted), 24. This is a 36-page booklet written and sold by Ndiaye to tourists visiting the island's slave museum and other memorial sites.

Chapter 6

1 Frantz Fanon, *Black Skins, White Masks*, (New York: Grove Press, 1967), 18.
2 Diallo, "Mauritania: The Other Apartheid?": 38.
3 As noted in a videotaped and audio-recorded interview with Messaoud Ould Boulkheir in Nouakchott, Mauritania, January 1996 (conducted by the author).
4 Boubacar Messaoud, *20 Questions on Slavery in Mauritania* (Nouakchott, Mauritania: Boubacar Messaoud, May 1995), 4.

5 Mark Fritz, "Rights of Ownership: Slavery's Lingering Hold on Mauritania" (New York: Associated Press, 8 August 1994).

Chapter 7

1 Comments made at the 13 March 1996 Committee on International Relations hearing on slavery in Mauritania and Sudan, Washington, D.C.
2 U.S. Department of State, *Country Reports on Human Rights Practices for 1994* (Washington, D.C.: U.S. Department of State, February 1995). Submitted to the Senate Committee on Foreign Relations and the House Committee on International Relations, 104th Congress, 1st Session.

Chapter 8

1 Quoted in Gordon, *Slavery in the Arab World*, 102.
2 Karl Marx, *The Eighteenth Brumaire of Louis Bonaparte* (New York: International Publishers, 1964).
3 Fanon, *Black Skins, White Masks*, 9.
4 Derrick Bell, *Faces at the Bottom of the Well* (New York: Basic Books, 1992), 1, 2.
5 Ibid., 3.
6 Ibid., 12.
7 Joseph E. Holloway, ed., *Africanisms in American Culture* (Bloomington, IN: Indiana University Press, 1990), 4, 5.
8 Letter to Benjamin F. Chavis, Jr., Executive Director of the National Association for the Advancement of Colored People, from the Honorable Frank R. Wolf (R–Virginia), 15 July 1993.
9 Letter to Chavis from Wolf, 19 August 1993.
10 Tim Sandler, "Striking at Slavery," *Boston Phoenix* (18 August 1995): 10.

Chapter 9

1 Albert Camus, *Resistance, Rebellion, and Death*, trans. Justin O'Brien (New York: Alfred A. Knopf, 1961), 26.